Simplifying Life

Simple Steps for Finding Your Way (in a Complex World)

Brett Taylor

Simplifying Life:
Simple Steps for Finding Your Way (in a Complex World)
by Brett Taylor

Editor: Glenn McMahan, Endeavor Literary Services, LLC
Cover and Interior design: Rebecca Finkel, F + P Graphic Design

Library of Congress Catalog Number: data on file

ISBN paper: 978-0-6482010-0-7
ISBN ebook: 978-0-6482010-1-4

Printed in the USA

Contents

Introduction

"Everything should be made as simple as possible,
but not one bit simpler."
—Albert Einstein

If I told you to chop your hand off would you do it? I hope not (we've only just met). What if I told you that great wisdom could be achieved from having your hand chopped off? Are you a little more tempted now? No? Me either.

The truth is, adversity can (and often does) bring great wisdom. You can acquire that wisdom in one of two ways:

1. Go through the adversity yourself to learn the lessons (sounds a little painful if it involves cutting off a limb, or parts thereof).

2. Listen to someone who's lived through adversity and learn the lessons from them.

Which seems most appealing to you? If you went for number two, then this is your lucky day. I've been blessed with a succession of challenging experiences that have given me more than a few unique insights. I'm happy to share those insights, and hopefully save you the inconvenience of acquiring them *single handedly*. (Cross my heart; there will be no other jokes that bad.)

Make no mistake.
If you read this book,
it WILL change your life.

Yeah, I know that's a big claim, but I can prove it. I've been writing this thing for over thirty years. I've bothered, browbeaten, and bored many friends and patients in that time with my ideas and perspectives. Ten years ago, the book was mostly finished, and I enlisted twelve people to formally beta-test my theories. I got comments like:

"This will make a difference for me and my life."

"This book has had a positive impact on my life; I plan to make it my constant companion."

"Your observations on what is really important in life are spot on, and your advice is second to none."

"Your book was fun to read. You definitely made me look closer at some of my faults that I was attributing to others. Not many folks can write that serious and that witty at the same time."

OK, I know what you're thinking. "If the book was that good back then, how come it took you another ten years to finish it?"

Yeah, that's a good question. In my defense, a lot has happened to me in the last ten years. Life got in the way of my writing about life (yes, the irony isn't lost on me either). The good news for you people reading now is that I have even more insights to share. It's a better book now, and I'm glad for the intervening challenges, and the fact it took a tad longer than anticipated to get done.

If I'm any judge, I suspect you have another question. The big one: "What am I going to learn?"

And a good question it is, too. You're going to learn how to cope better with the maelstrom that is modern life. The pressure of living increases day-by-day. For all the marvels of technology, life isn't getting any easier; in fact, it's getting harder. There's too much information, there's too much happening, and there are too many demands on our time and attention. The pages ahead are my cookbook for getting your shit together (as the young people like to say), for simplifying and prioritizing your life.

For three decades, I've held everything that's happened to me up to the proverbial looking glass and pondered the question, "What's really important?" It's amazing how clearly you can think with the prospect of death hanging over your head (don't try it at home, kids). Let me share with you, as succinctly as possible, what I've learned and what I think you need to do to get your life on track. I think you're going to enjoy the ride.

A Little Orientation

Life is a journey. A vast, long, single-destination trip filled with adventure, risk, and reward. You have to believe that at the very core of your being. My central premise (and it's a very simple central premise) is that everything that happens (good or bad) on your journey happens for a reason. Whatever happens to you is useful (even if you don't think so at the time). Everything gives you an opportunity to learn something. If you take the alternative view, that life has no rhyme or reason, then you're forced into being a victim of circumstances beyond your control. If you subscribe to my viewpoint, then "bad" things happen to teach you lessons. If the "bad" thing is going to happen anyway, you may as well treat it as a positive and learn something so that some good comes from the bad.

The more astute among you will have determined what the "single destination" of your life is. As this book goes to press, all of us are going to die someday. That may change in the future, but it's the current reality. I don't want you to focus on dying, however. I want you to focus on maximizing your enjoyment of all the things that happen between now and when you do shuffle off.

Trans-American Journey Analogy

I've always wanted to drive across the United States, from Los Angeles to New York (taking the scenic route of course). I love the idea of an epic journey. To help you focus on the epic journey that is your life, I want you to think of this book (and your life) like it's a trip across the US—an adventure-filled trip that will be a little more enjoyable, and a little more hassle-free, if you engage in some judicious preparation and planning. I'm going to relate each section of the book to this trip, to help you think like your life is a journey. So, it goes something like this (well, *exactly* like this):

- **Section 1** is about how you should prepare for the journey (tidying up loose ends, putting your mental house in order, cleaning the massive squashed bug that has been distracting you for years off your car windshield).

- **Section 2** is about picking a destination and planning the journey.

- **Section 3** is about how you should behave on the journey (the road rules, if you like).

- **Section 4** deals with road hazards to look out for, such as pot holes, speed bumps, wombat crossings, volcanic lava flows, etc.

- **Section 5** gives you strategies for dealing with those problems if they occur (advanced driver training).

- And **Section 6** is about who you might meet on the journey.

Other things you need to know before we go on:
If you read this book and don't change a single thing in your life, then I've been a complete failure and will likely end up in author hell.

To make it as easy as possible for you to apply my principles (and keep me out of literary purgatory), I've summarized the entire book on one page. Obviously, you have to read from start to finish before it makes sense, but once you have, the single page will serve as your cheat sheet. You can download the single-page summary at my website (*www. simplifyinglife.me*) which will also serve as a living and growing appendix to the book. In addition, the website will help you keep track of your goals. More on that later.

This book has a split personality. It's part story, part recipe book, and part homework. It's not supposed to be a passive experience. If you just read it as an intellectual exercise and don't test the principles, you won't get the full experience. You can read a recipe in a cookbook and imagine what the food will taste like, or you can go to the trouble of making the recipe and actually find out. There's a big difference.

So, the decision is yours: Passively imagine what your life could be like, or take a little time and effort and find out.

Let's get started. How well can you remove that big squashed bug off the windshield of your life? Let's see.

Section 1

Making Peace
with the Past
(Preparations for the Journey)

"This is not theory.
This is your life we're talking about."
—Brett Taylor (me)

Wherever you are in life, the future is your journey. If you were going on an actual journey, you'd get your house in order before you left, right? You'd put the garbage out, get the pets boarded, cancel the milk, turn off the lights, close the windows, lock the doors, and do all the other mundane stuff necessary to allow you to go away unburdened with worrying about "little things."

Well, it's the same with the journey ahead that is your life. I want you to undertake this trip with a clear head. Experience tells me, however, that there are a lot of heads out there that aren't particularly clear. If yours is one of them, then we need to fix that.

Too many people go through life with too much mental baggage. Mental baggage is like a clock-radio alarm going off in the next room. You can mostly block out the annoying buzzing sound, but you always know it's there, and you always know it should be turned off.

The way I see it, there are two sorts of mental baggage we need to deal with to prepare for your journey. The two categories are:

1. Damaged relationships with others

2. Damaged relationships with ourselves

Be Warned:
There May Be Pain Ahead.

Let me mix metaphors here to make my point. (I love a good metaphor mixing . . . it keeps you on your toes.) Reading a book about weightlifting won't make you any stronger. You need to start lifting for that to happen. If all you do is passively read the following section, nothing will happen. To get any benefit from the book, you have to actively participate. *You have to do what I suggest no matter how hard it seems.* "No pain no gain" as the sweaty people like to say. Some of you will be in good mental shape already. Some of you may suffer a little discomfort. No one, however, will die.

OK, take a deep breath and let's do this!

1.1 Damaged Relationships with Others

a) Parents and Children

There are three distinct periods in your life: Dependence, Independence, and Interdependence. The Dependence period is from birth to about puberty. Babies and young children are completely dependent on their parents. There is a great deal of love both ways. It is a wonderful, simple(ish) time.

Then there's the Independence phase. This is from about puberty to sometime in your 20s or beyond. Children/adolescents start exercising their own wills and making their own decisions. Parents during this period can be somewhat of a hindrance to the process. Adolescents expect a twenty-four-hour maid and limousine service, but they don't necessarily value those services.

The Interdependence phase begins the moment you start appreciating your parents again. There's an old joke that pretty much sums it up: "When I was seventeen and living at home, dad and I used to fight all of the time. We'd never agree on anything. Now I'm thirty-seven with kids of my own and we seem to agree on everything. It's amazing how much he's learned in the last twenty years."

The Problem

You love your children to death. Most parents would take a bullet for their kids. It's not until you have children of your own that you truly appreciate how much your own parents love/loved you.

I didn't have my first child until I was forty, so I had plenty of time to dislike those condescending, "holier than thou" types who had already spawned, who were always quick to opine: "You'll understand when you have children of your own." If you don't have children, you will know exactly what I'm talking about, and you'll dislike these people just as much as I did. The annoying thing, however, is that those people were right. You really need kids of your own to understand the circle of life.

Anyway, because you love your kids so much, and because it's obvious to you how much you love them, you can easily overlook the need to tell them you love them when they're little.

I took my first daughter, Lauren, over to visit my grandmother one day. Lauren was two and Granny was ninety-two. As we were leaving, Granny said, "I love you, Lauren." I was amazed by how shocked and uncomfortable that made me feel. I quickly figured out how I had been snared by a common trap.

So, this is how it happens. You love your kids so much that you don't feel you need to tell them, or don't tell them very often. When they enter the Independence phase, the last thing they want to hear is mum and dad say, "I love you," and saying that may not be on their to-do list either. By the time they pass through the teenage tunnel, the whole "love" thing becomes an awkward issue on both sides.

Now I'm not saying this happens to everyone, but I've discussed this theory with enough people that I've come to the conclusion that it's a common (and way underdiagnosed) problem. You unaffected people who think this is "much ado about nothing" can just tag along for a few pages feeling smug about how superior you are.

Let's Test My Theory

There's a very simple way to see if this problem affects you or not. If you have living parents or children, grab a phone now, call them, and tell them that you love them. If you're reaching for your phone, you don't have a problem. If you're thinking to yourself, "They know I love them, I don't have to do this," then you have a problem. I'm serious. If you're making excuses not to do it, then you have issues, and they need to be addressed.

This Is the Real Problem

There is nothing more fundamental in life than the relationships between you and your parents, and between your kids and you. These relationships are easily strained during the Independence phase of life. If they don't get sorted out afterwards, you're doomed to a life that is somehow lacking. Something will always be missing. Your life will feel faintly unsatisfying, despite whatever success you might enjoy. You need to sort these relationships out before you can fully live your life.

In discussing this idea with lots of people, I've concluded that those who struggle with the "I love you" thing fall into two categories:

1. Those who immediately see it's an issue, but are scared to address it

2. Those who are in denial and dismiss its importance

For those in the first category, I'm going to try to help you. For those in the second category, I ask you to ponder whether you think your parents and/or children would like to hear you tell them that you love them. If the answer is yes, why would you deny them that?

The Solution

The solution is to just do it, no matter how hard or awkward you think it's going to be. Don't just take my word for it, though. This is the experience of Mike, a dentist mate of mine and one of the book's early beta testers. Mike told me this:

I have to relate a story about the first chapter. I was sitting delayed in an airport trying to get home. I was in a foul mood and I start reading your book. And of course, what do I get first thing: 'Tell your mother you love her.' Oh great. Thanks a lot, Brett. My dad is no problem, but anyone who knows my mom will tell you that she is a challenging individual. My phone conversations with her usually run about five minutes, three of which are total silence on my end. So, when the first thing I had to do was call up and say 'I love you,' that didn't exactly thrill me. Well, I sucked it up for Brett and rang her up. I kind of beat around the bush for a while and talked about how my kids were really becoming a handful as late teens with boyfriends, etc. And then I said, 'I know I probably don't really say it much, and I was probably a challenge when I was a teen back then, too, but I really appreciate all you did for me and I love you for it.' I can barely believe I got it out of my mouth. Well, she didn't register shock or anything like I thought she might, but we proceeded to have a very pleasant fifty-minute phone conversation. She ended up telling me some stories about a vacation she took when she was a kid that I had never even heard in all the years previously. You have to understand that this is a woman whom I can usually tolerate about five minutes of phone conversation with at the most. The 'I love you' really did make a big difference. I even said it again at the end of the conversation, and it was easier the second time.

Thanks Mike. Great work. Now, what about the rest of you affected types. What are you waiting for? You could have an outcome similar to Mike's in a matter of moments with one simple phone call. All the people who have taken the "I love you" challenge tell me it feels like a weight has been lifted from their shoulders.

I get on very well with my own parents. We've never had any serious family disputes. I would consider us to be a normal, happy family. Probably happier than most. When I figured out how important this whole "I love you mum and dad" thing was, I decided to take the test myself. You see, I'm talking from experience here. I love my parents, but the thought of telling them that somehow terrified me, and I had no idea why. I decided I wasn't allowed to continue writing the book until I told them I love them. But how does a grown man tell his father (he was the hardest for me) he loves him?

It was like being an awkward teenager again. Remember asking someone out on a date? Man, I used to hate that. I'd feel sick every time. Well, that's how I felt when I decided I had to tell Dad I loved him, only a lot worse. And let me tell you, it's stupid. Sure, the girl might say no, but how is a parent going to respond?

What Happened?

I'm glad you asked. I can sense your voyeuristic desire to savor my discomfort. You have to appreciate that at that point in time I was very early in my understanding of the problem. In the interests of research, I decided that if I was going to make you people do it, then I had to find out exactly how hard it could be.

I picked a time when Dad and I were alone and not likely to be interrupted. I used a strategy called preposterous overestimation to make it a little easier. You probably do it all the time. It's when you say to someone, "I've got a really, really, really big favor to ask." They think you want them to help you move pianos all weekend and then you say, "Can you lend me five dollars?" You over dramatize the situation to make the reality less severe. I taught my team members this and now they use it on me all the time, so be careful.

So, I said to Dad, "I've got something really difficult to tell you." Now I was nervous as hell and my voice was quivering, so I'm sure that helped the effect. My father feared the worst and confronted me with his greatest fear: "You're not going to tell me you're gay, are you?" (You just have to love that homophobic generation.) I said, "No, I'm writing a book and I need to tell you how much I love you and how much I appreciate everything you've done for me over the years." He replied, "I love you and Kerry, too." (Kerry's my sister.)

With the ice broken, the conversation was a lot easier, and I learned more about Dad in the next ten minutes than I had in the previous forty-odd years.

Breaking the Ice

Now, the more astute among you will have realized that I didn't actually tell him I loved him. It was a cop-out. I blamed the book. I had to tell him because of the book. And he said he loved me *and* my sister. He copped-out, too. By lumping me in with her it made it easier for him. None of that matters though. Once you break through the ice, the rest is easy.

It's Better than Being Sick

In Western societies, you normally wait for your parents to become terminally ill before telling them you love them. Once you know they're going to die, suddenly the imperative to come clean with your emotions outweighs the fear of doing it. You always hear people talking about how wonderful a parent's death was because they could say so many things and connect so well before the end. So why wait for someone to be sick? It's stupidity. And what if they die suddenly? Then you miss the chance altogether.

Third Party Help

Ok, so I've convinced you to do it, but you still think it's going to be hard. Here's the easiest approach. I call it "third-party help." Basically, you blame someone else for your actions. It's a little dishonest, but it breaks the ice and gets the job done.

So, you ring your mother and the conversation goes something like this: "Mum, I bought this book today and I'm not allowed to read the second chapter until I tell you how much I love you. The book's expensive considering how small it is, so I don't have any options. Mum, I love you."

Now Mum will be happy to hear this despite the disclaimer (mothers are like that). Once you get it out in the open you should be able to say it again without the book helping you. It's only hard to do the first time. It should get a lot easier very quickly and eventually be very natural.

Of course, once this book is an international bestseller, mothers around the world will be expecting the phone call, which will make saying I love you a whole lot easier; but if you're an early adopter, you'll need a little more gumption.

I admit I copped-out big time when I did this with my own mother. The conversation went something like this: "Mum, I'm writing an international bestseller and I can't write the second chapter until I tell you how much I love you." Then I hopped in my car and drove off. Sure, she was confused, but I got the message across.

If a phone call is too uncomfortable, then let technology be your friend. Use the same strategy with a text message or an e-mail. Still use the third-party help tactic if you need to. So, an e-mail would be something like this: "Mum, I'm reading this book and I can't read the second chapter until I tell you I love you (and I do). What's for dinner tonight?"

Break the ice. That's the key. Then up the ante until you get everything off your chest. So, your options are:

1. **Text message or e-mail** (as above)

2. **Phone call:** If you went for the e-mail/text message plan first, then the phone call should go like this: "Mum, I've read a little more of the book and apparently I have to tell you in person that I love you." Just keep blaming the book to make it easier.

3. **Say it face-to-face:** If it's still too uncomfortable, then make it an afterthought. You know, say, "Love you, Mum" as you're walking out the door. Do that every time you see your parents until it's easy.

4. **The proper "I love you":** You might be able to do this quickly, or it may take some time. Eventually, you want to have a conversation about it. After you've broken the ice it shouldn't be too stressful.

Difficult Situations

A lot of you might have deceased parents. If you were lucky, you had the "I love you" conversation before your parents died. But if they died suddenly, maybe you didn't. Your solution is easy. Let go. Yes, you probably have regrets, and yes, there are a lot of things you wish you said (or didn't say), but it isn't going to happen, so you need to move on. Get a picture of your parent and say out loud, "I love you." Have a little cry if you want, but get it out of your system.

If your parents did something nasty to you, it's important to acknowledge that you loved them very much at one time. I heard the actor and comedian Billy Connolly discuss the fact that his father sexually abused him as a child. He strongly made the point that he loved his father and forgave him for what he did. He also said that it wasn't any of his business why his father abused him. I took that to mean he didn't blame himself, and that he couldn't know why his father did it. It was separate from their "normal" loving relationship. He loved his father for all the happy times, and forgave him for whatever it was in his past, or whatever sickness was going on in his brain that had made his father abuse him. It seemed like a very sensible way of dealing with a difficult situation. I doubt most people could be that pragmatic. It was inspiring.

Not everyone is a great parent. Not everyone is a good person. Good or bad, however, at some point every child loves his or her parents. Even if your mum and dad didn't love you, you loved them. Nothing can change that. You can't ignore the fact that you loved them, even if you wished you could. It happened. And if they didn't deserve that love, then you need to acknowledge that and move on.

Let me quote Billy Connolly (who was abandoned by his mother at age three, in addition to being abused by his father) on how to deal with a difficult childhood: "You have to put it behind you. You don't have a choice. If you don't you are condemned to be defined by it and carry it around like a big rucksack full of rocks. Nobody tells you you can put it down and walk away, but you can."

He really is a very inspiring man.

Planning for the Future

All this angst created by trying to re-establish relationships with your parents could easily be prevented by parents not allowing barriers to develop in the first place. It's something you need to do if you are a parent. Once I got over the shock and embarrassment of my grandmother telling my daughter she loved her, I thought, "There's a good idea." Now I tell my two daughters I love them every single day, sometimes a couple of times a day. I plan to do that every day through tears, tantrums, giggles, and guffaws. If I don't let a barrier develop, then they won't have to spend any emotional energy on breaking one down (with me) in the future. Telling them that I love them is now the easiest, most natural thing in the world. It's almost like I can't remember how awkward it first was. There are few better things you can do for a child growing up than making them feel loved and wanted.

If your children are grown up and you haven't told them that you love them in a long time (or maybe ever) then it's time to person-up and do it. All the strategies for tackling the problem with parents can be used for breaking the ice with grown children. You can never have enough love in your life. It doesn't matter how old you are, you'll always be glad to hear a parent say "I love you."

It's Not Always that Simple

We all know relationships can be complex. Just telling someone you love them isn't guaranteed to fix everything if there's a lot going on. It's an essential start, but it's not a panacea. Sometimes it's necessary to apologize for past transgressions (words and actions). Sometimes it's necessary to forgive past transgressions. You can't change the past, but you can alter the future. A wounded relationship can heal given the right conditions. If you desire a relationship with a parent or child to be improved, just start somewhere. Do something to kick the process off (a gift, a kind word, a kind gesture). I'm not saying it's easy, and I'm not saying it's guaranteed to work, but if you don't try something, then nothing will happen.

OK, we've addressed parents and children. Let's move on to other people in our lives.

b) Other Family and Friends

I know too many people with too many damaged relationships, and, frankly, I think it's stupid. I know spouses who don't express love to each other. I know people who choose to have no contact with their children, and even have grandchildren they've never met. And of course, those grandchildren have never had the opportunity to love their grandparent. I know people who don't see their siblings because of petty, mostly forgotten arguments. I know best mates who have fallen out over nothing.

It's all needless, correctable stupidity. Now, having said that, if in your heart-of-hearts you're truly happy with a severed relationship and it doesn't nag at you in some tiny part of your brain, then you might be OK. A more likely scenario is that in some small way you regret the fact that an important relationship is damaged. If that's the case, then set about repairing it. If it's impossible to repair (because the person has died), or if it can't be repaired even though you've tried your hardest, then let it go.

You don't get to take excess baggage on your journey. It slows you down too much. Fix what needs fixing. You can do it. I know you can.

Last but not least, there is one person you are closer to than all others. Any clue who I'm talking about?

1.2 Damaged Relationships with Ourselves

It's hard to live a perfect life. In fact, I can make a case that it's counterproductive. I mean, how can you learn things without making mistakes?

Mistakes lead to detours, and it's on the road less travelled that you see the best scenery. Some mistakes, however, are bigger than others. You may have made a few in your life that still gnaw at you, mistakes that you're having a hard time getting over.

Let me tell you one of mine. It may make you feel a little better about a few of yours. This mistake could kill me one day, so I think we can all agree it's significant.

About ten years ago, I found a lump in my neck. I don't recall exactly how I found it; shaving, I guess. One day it wasn't there and the next day it was. I didn't pay much attention to it because it didn't hurt, and it didn't seem to get any bigger. In retrospect, I know this was stupid, but that's the definition of a mistake, isn't it? In my defense, I did ask a few medical colleagues in passing what they thought it was, but I never followed up on their sensible suggestions to get it properly checked. Then my mate Chris got cancer in his throat and had half his neck cut out. That scared me a little. I was sure my lump was nothing, but thanks to Chris I felt I had to find out what the hell it was. I just couldn't live with the nagging fear any longer.

I expect you can see where this story is going. Turns out my lump was cancer, and not a very nice one either. The oncologist reassured me I had a 95 percent chance of living five years. I didn't tell him it had been there five years already, so I'd already squandered that time. My long-term prospects were less rosy. Dr. Google kindly informed me that I had a 30 percent chance of living fifteen years. Not great odds. As I write this, it's twelve years since the timer started.

So, what's my point? Not getting the lump checked was a mistake. It was a mistake that could kill me. It was a mistake that could prevent me from seeing my little girls grow up. It was a mistake that could deny my wife a partner in her old age. It was a mistake that could deny some little kids in the future the enjoyment of having a grandfather. Put simply, it was a big fucking mistake! (Excuse my Australian.) But what are my options? Mistakes can't be unmade. I can either live my life tormented by something I have no way of changing (carrying around Billy's rucksack of rocks), or I can let it go and get on with living. It's a simple decision (well, I think it's simple).

Putting my life-threatening stupidity aside, I see lots of people beating themselves up over missed opportunities. It's easy to think your life could have or should have amounted to something more, to feel that you haven't fulfilled your potential. Maybe you dreamed of being a writer but became a dentist instead. (Hang on, I know that guy.) Or you made financial mistakes, or business mistakes, or property purchase mistakes (been there), or you never asked out the girl you loved and wonder how your life may have been different if you had. (I dodged that one.)

Life is full of what-ifs and maybes. I like the cosmology theory that says there is an infinite number of universes and realities. In one of those realities, maybe there is a version of another you, one who didn't make any mistakes. How cool is that? Or . . . How boring must that guy/gal be? Most people in this universe (the one where I wrote my book) can't do everything right.

Remember my central premise about learning from mistakes? If you never make a mistake, how do you learn anything? You don't learn things when you're right. You learn things when you're wrong. No, I don't want you to risk leaving your kids as orphans by making my stupid mistake on purpose. I hope you learn from my mistake (which is why I bothered mentioning it). Making mistakes is not the problem. Carrying those mistakes with you through life (like Billy's rocks) is the problem. You have to *forgive yourself* for the mistakes you've made. It's very important to do that, and to mean it.

Do you have any mistakes that haunt you? Something you desperately wish you could change? Guess what? It's not going to happen. You can't change the past, but you can change the future (I keep saying that, so it must be important). It's pointless wasting energy on second-guessing the past. Let it go.

Trans-American Journey Analogy

I have likened life to a grand journey. Well, making peace with the past is like getting your car ready for the trip. It's putting your house in order, cancelling the milk and papers, turning off the iron. It's cleaning the squashed bug off the windshield of your life so you can see the road ahead clearly. You won't enjoy the scenery if all you do is look in the rearview mirror.

in summary

- Tell your parents (dead or alive) that you love them.
- Tell your children (dead or alive) that you love them.
- Tell your spouse/partner that you love them (if you do).
- Repair relationships with friends and other family.
- Accept and forgive all your past mistakes and move on.
- Make your peace with the past.

Section 2

Goals
(Choosing a Destination)

So, how'd you do? Have you made peace with the past? If you have, ink in a big smiley face next to that section on the summary sheet at the back of the book (e-book users resist that urge), and give yourself a pat on the back. I hope you're feeling proud, and maybe even a little bit smug. If you haven't, I'd like to respectfully suggest you stop now and ponder why. Getting your mental house in order is an important part of your life journey.

Just reading a cookbook when you're hungry achieves nothing. You're still going to be hungry. You need to take action to feed your stomach, and you need to take action to feed your soul.

If the reason you haven't been able to make peace with the past is that the previous section has uncovered something you can't face alone, then please seek professional help. We can't do everything in life by ourselves. You wouldn't take your appendix out by yourself, would you? Mental health is no different. There is no shame in asking for help. Find a good doctor, discuss your situation, and allow them to point you in the right direction. This is what these people (happily) do for a living. Take advantage of them.

OK, let's continue getting the rest of this life of yours organized. I know you're busy, but I want things wrapped up by lunch. Please go and get a pencil now. Don't ask questions, just do it, and keep it close by while you're reading. You've got work to do.

Right, so where are we now? I'll tell you. You've stabilized the foundations, you've made your bed, you've cleared the deck, you've wiped the slate clean, you've washed the squashed bug off the windshield of your life. The road ahead is clear, but which road?

2.1 Goal Setting

Everyone knows they should have written goals. Hands up if yours are written down. Yes, that's what I thought. Setting goals is a great idea in principle, but not enough people even have goals, let alone write them down. Well, that's about to change (for you at least). We're going to make it simple, so you DO it.

Do you know why you're supposed to write your goals down? There's a great book called *Influence* by Robert Cialdini. One of the things he writes about is a concept called Commitment and Consistency. In a nutshell, your brain is hardwired so that if you say you're going to do something, you are more likely to do it. It seems to be an evolutionary advantage. Writing a goal down is a way of reminding yourself that you made a commitment, and so you are more likely to follow through on that commitment. Anyway, the bottom line is that you HAVE to have goals and you HAVE to write them down. Again, this is not optional. If you're not going to do it, stop reading now and give this book to someone more motivated. You can read a comic instead. This stuff is not theory. You need to apply it.

OK, enough chastising. If you're still here, you probably agree with me that goals are a good thing. If you've never had written goals before, it was probably because you didn't know what you wanted. It's like when my wife asks me what I want for dinner. I don't know, what are my options?

What's Important?

I think the three most important things in life are family, health, and career, in that order. We're going to establish goals in these three areas first. This is not supposed to be a complicated exercise. Don't stress about what to write down. You can always change your mind later. As you achieve your goals, you'll need new ones anyway, so just write something down.

I'm a big believer in reaching for the stars so that maybe you can touch the moon. You have to extend yourself when goal setting. Your first goal in each category will be an unrealistic long-term goal. A good test to see if it's unrealistic is to tell it to someone. They should either laugh at you or think you're crazy. This type of goal isn't just a stretch, it's almost impossible. It can't actually be impossible, but it should be close.

Why an "Unrealistic" Goal?

Why do you need an unrealistic long-term goal? Because you don't know how good you are. You can't know your limits until you test them. Many years ago, it was commonly believed that the four-minute mile was unachievable. It was "beyond the limits of human endurance." So how did they test to see if that was true? By giving it a go, that's how. If no one had ever set about trying to break the four-minute mile, we'd never know if it was possible. If you don't set goals beyond what you think is reasonable to achieve, you'll never know what your limits are. Great things are achieved because great people ignore the naysayers and set about trying to achieve the impossible. If you don't try, you'll never know how great you are, will you?

So, remember, people should laugh at your unrealistic long-term goal. My unrealistic long-term career goal is for this book to be the second best-selling book of all time. Do you think I'm crazy? Good. Is my goal impossible? No, just very unlikely. I won't know if it's impossible until I give it a go. And in the process of attempting the "impossible," I'll achieve a lot more than if I'd just set a mundane goal.

Your next goal in each category is a *realistic* long-term goal. This should be something you can actually achieve with a lot of hard work. If you tell friends this goal they should nod their heads and agree that you might be able to do that. This goal should not be so easy that it's a "slam dunk," but something that is possible with considerable determination. My realistic long-term career goal is to get this book published. Not a lot of people get books published, but no one's going to tell me I'm mad for trying.

Your last goal in each category is a realistic short-term goal. This will be your road map to achieving the realistic long-term goal. This goal will change often as you head off toward the realistic long-term goal. To make your realistic short-term goal even more realistic and easier to attain, I want you to break it down into four sections:

1. One day

2. One week

3. One month

4. Next birthday

So, what do you have to do by this time tomorrow to take the first step toward your realistic long-term goal? What will you achieve by next week? What will you achieve by next month? What will you achieve by your next birthday? I like the birthday idea because it's a date you're not going to forget, and most of us like to think we've achieved something since our last birthday (apart from a few extra pounds); otherwise all we've been doing is getting older. Every birthday, go through the process again and reset your goals. If you get stuck along the way reset your goals starting with the one-day goal. I don't want you to have a one-day goal every day; that starts to get a little ridiculous. But if things go off the rails (you are likely to a have a few detours in life, so don't stress about it), then just start from the beginning. No harm done.

So, my one-day career realistic short-term goal in writing this book might be to buy a pencil. In case you're wondering, my short-term goals for the book before it was published were:

1. Take the chapter 1 challenge

2. Write an outline

3. Complete chapter 1

4. Write a chapter a month for the next four months

5. Get the first draft done

6. Get the second draft done

7. Test my ideas on a bunch of unsuspecting friends

8. Find a literary agent

9. Give up on the literary agent idea

10. Find a great editor (hi Glenn)

11. Review editing

12. Find a great cover designer (hi Rebecca)

13. Find a great website guy (hi Steve)

14. Publish the book myself

And that's where I'm at now.

Just Do It

I don't want you to stretch yourself too far to get started. A common problem with goal-setting is that the destination is so far away that the whole journey seems too onerous; so, nothing happens. The trick is to take one step. Do one thing, not two, just one. Under no circumstances feel obligated to do two things. Your one-day realistic short-term goal should be very realistic and very achievable. It's designed to get you started and to build your confidence. The trick is to just do it, which is what we're about to do.

At the end of the book is a summary with spaces to fill in. If you're reading an electronic version of the book, or you're one of those obsessive-compulsive types who wouldn't fold a page corner as a book mark, let alone write something (heaven forbid), then, go to *www.simplifyinglife.me* and print out a summary page to write on. Of course, if you're a "living on the wild side" sort of person, you can just write your goals in the pages below. OK, now, grab that pencil in your sweaty little fingers and get ready to have a lot of fun.

Remember the cookbook analogy? Reading recipes doesn't get you fed. Likewise, just reading the following bit won't change anything. You have to write something down now if you want anything in your life to change.

To help you, I've filled in my goals, but get some of your own. And if for some inexplicable reason your goals are the same as mine, I still want you to write them down. Also, write the deadline after each short-term goal.

Family

Unrealistic Long-Term Goal

Brett: My kids writing a book about how great a father I am

You: _____

Realistic Long-Term Goal

Brett: One big trip a year with the kids between now and when they finish school

You: _____

Realistic Short-Term Goal

Brett:

1 Day: Discuss holiday idea with my wife (date)

1 Week: Identify destinations and time of year that is feasible (date)

1 Month: Block off work schedule and book first holiday (date)

Birthday: First holiday will be booked and taken, repeat process

You:

One day: _____ Date: _____

One week: _____ Date: _____

One month: _____ Date: _____

Birthday: _____

Health

Unrealistic Long-Term Goal

Brett: Mountain bike riding at age 110

You: _____

Realistic Long-Term Goal

Brett: 85kg (187 pounds) with muscles by end of next year

You: _____

Realistic Short-Term Goal:

Brett:

1 day: Pump up bike tires (date)

1 week: Plan exercise schedule (date)

1 month: Exercise schedule fully implemented (date)

Birthday: 90kg

You:

One day: _____ Date: _____

One week: _____ Date: _____

One month: _____ Date: _____

Birthday: _____

Career

Unrealistic Long-Term Goal

Brett: Write the second best-selling book of all time

You: _____

Realistic Long-Term Goal

Brett: Getting this book published

You: _____

Realistic Short-Term Goal

Brett:

1 day: Finish this bit (date)

1 week: Half way through revising Glenn's edit (date)

1 month: Finish revising first edit (date)

Birthday: Self-publish if no bastard signs me up (date)

You:

One day: _____ Date: _____

One week: _____ Date: _____

One month: _____ Date: _____

Birthday: _____

Continuing Support

I've read a lot of great books over the years, with lots of great ideas that I wanted to implement. Sadly, most of those ideas are still sitting in those books on a dusty shelf somewhere. Sound like anyone you know, or is it just me?

I want this book to be different and I've got a plan. If you go to my website, *www.simplifyinglife.me,* you can write your goals down in cyberspace. Through the genius of modern technology I will be riding your ass to make sure you constantly focus on your goals and achieve the dreams I want you to have. This book might get dusty, but your goals and dreams wont.

Other Important Things

We're going to discuss the concept of spirituality at the end of chapter 6. If you wish to include spiritual goals under health, that's fine with me (it is mental health, after all), but we will be looking at that from another angle later.

Don't feel limited by the categories I've given you. You can have multiple goals in each category, or you can create your own categories.

SMART Goals

You may have heard that goals should be SMART. Here's a definition I stole off the Internet about SMART goals. The first meaning for each letter is the one I prefer, and the others are alternatives:

S specific (also significant, stretching)

M measurable (also meaningful, motivational)

A acceptable (also attainable, agreed upon, action-oriented, achievable)

R realistic (also relevant, reasonable, rewarding, results-oriented)

T timely (also time-based, tangible, trackable)

SMART goals are just a way of analyzing your goals to make them more achievable. Your unrealistic long-term goals do not have to be SMART. Think of them as a dream. Your realistic long-term goals should be SMART, however. Let's take one of mine and see if it's SMART.

Health: Realistic long-term goal—85 kg (187 pounds) with muscles by end of next year.

Specific: It's somewhat specific. If I'd said I wanted to be healthier that wouldn't be specific, but I've picked weight out of the health barrel, so that's good. The muscles bit, however, isn't very specific.

Measurable: You want a goal you can measure so you know if you've achieved it. Yes, 85 kg is measurable, but the muscles bit isn't. That part of my goal is starting to look lame (like my muscles at the moment).

Acceptable: An acceptable goal means it's something you want. There is no point having a goal if it's not your goal. So, if you're wife buys you ten lessons with a personal trainer named Cindy who pushes you within an inch of your worthless life and makes your every waking moment a misery beyond description and you don't really want to be there, well, that's not going to be an acceptable goal, is it? My wife on the other hand loves spending time with Cindy. Anyway, pick goals you actually want to achieve. Is my goal acceptable? Well, it is; it's something I want to do.

Realistic: Like I said before, I want your realistic long-term goal to be realistic. The more astute among you have probably figured that out already. (Give yourself another pat on the back; you could have written this book yourself.) So, this goal has to be doable. Can I really get down to 85 kg AND get a few muscles? I think I can.

Timely: This means give yourself a deadline. Nothing airy-fairy. If you're going to do it, figure out when you're going to do it. My goal is timely because I know my deadline.

So, how'd I do? Only fair, I'd say. The muscle thing let me down. It's not very specific. And while I could measure my biceps to make it more specific, I know I'm not going to do that, so that wouldn't make it acceptable. I could remove the muscle bit and that would make the weight part perfect, but I'm going to leave it in to remind myself to get more muscle.

So, what's the point of all this self-analysis? Don't get too obsessed about how **SMART** your goals are. You're better off having a goal in any form, **SMART** or not, than not having a goal just because you can't make it **SMART** enough.

Having goals is the smart part, making them **SMART** is just smarter. (The **SMART** goals section above was first written some years back. As we almost go to publication, I'm 86 kg and actually DO have muscles. I've almost achieved my realistic long-term health goal. This goal-setting shit actually works!!!)

Goal Buddies

Remember how we talked about commitment and consistency, and about how writing your goals down makes you more likely to follow through with them? Well, let's take that a step further. I want you to get a goal buddy, and I want you to share your goals with that person. Make sure you pick a hard-nosed goal buddy, someone who will pester you to stay on track. You will be more likely to achieve your goals if a third party keeps reminding you about them.

My goal buddy is Ronan Lutman, my business coach. He's not too hard-nosed, but he does a good job of keeping me accountable. Find someone who's reading the book, if you can, so they get the idea of what's going on. I want them riding you hard and putting you away wet, pretty much the way I'm treating you about all the things in the book. Do you think I'm going to make you write down who you're going to ask to be your goal buddy? Well, you're right.

Your goal buddy is:_____

Conveniently the Internet has come along since I first started writing the book. How lucky is that? If you haven't done so already, go to *www. simplifyinglife.me* and register. You can set your goals online, and take advantage of a cyber goal buddy who won't forget what you committed to do, and when you committed to do it by. This stuff works if you bother to do it, so bother to do it!

Visualization (Making Your Dreams Reality)

This is the coolest part of the book. Your brain can be a little bit gullible at times. Your subconscious doesn't know the difference between reality and imagination, and you can use that fact for good not evil. The process is very simple. It's so simple in fact that I expect you to do it on your back in bed with your eyes closed.

Each night as you go to sleep, I want you to visualize your three, unrealistic long-term goals. I want you to imagine them as if they are real. What does it look like? What does it feel like? How would people respond to you if it happened? Change the dreams around or stick with the same ones, it doesn't matter. What DOES matter is seeing in your mind's eye the things you want to achieve as if they are actually happening. If you aren't very good at this sort of thing, then imagine them as if they have already happened. Or pretend you are remembering a news story on TV featuring your goals and dreams (different stories for each dream and goal, obviously).

I'll share a few of my career dreams with you (the things I visualize each night that tell me I have achieved my unrealistic long-term goal). The main one (for the book) is imagining myself being interviewed by Oprah Winfrey. I know she's retired from her TV show. That's how long I've been writing this damned book. I figure that if she comes out of retirement just to interview me, I'll be well on my way to having the second best-selling book of all time. I also imagine myself getting the Nobel Peace Prize because some of the ideas in the book make the world such a better place to live in. And the last one is to imagine myself being so famous that Bruce Springsteen wants to write a few songs with me (I love Bruce).

Yes, I know my dreams are a bit corny, but we all enjoy imagining better futures for ourselves. Rather than imagining yourself winning the lottery, don't you think it would be better to set a process in place that gives you a real shot at achieving your dreams?

Your brain is a wonderful thing. It works behind your back, so to speak, solving the problems you give it. If you tell your brain something is true, it believes you. Soon you start acting more like the things you believe. What sort of a dad do you think I am day to day when I've been imagining my kids writing books about me? It works in the reverse, too, so keep those negative thoughts to a minimum (we'll discuss that later).

If you can visualize something happening, you make it more likely to happen. This is a well-used technique among elite sportsmen. Jack Nicklaus (the great golfer) sees every golf shot he hits in his mind's eye as a color movie before he hits it. It's a simple but very powerful technique that is easy to master, and essential to achieving success.

The subconscious mind makes up 92 percent of the brain. The other 8 percent is the conscious mind. It's the subconscious that does all the work. It's the subconscious mind that works without you thinking. Thinking (when you are aware that you are thinking) is your conscious mind. If you tell your subconscious what you want, it will set about achieving it for you.

There are lots of fancy ways to do this, but the simplest is as I've described: visualizing what you want as you fall asleep. It will allow you to convince yourself beyond any doubt that wonderful things are going to happen. It is very cool.

Remember: Reach for the stars. If you only touch the moon, that's a result we can both live with. If you never stretch yourself, however, you'll never know how far you can reach.

Life is a journey not a destination. I'm sure you've heard that before. Getting there is generally more fun than the being there. It's often hard to remember that, but make sure you do. It is one of life's great truisms.

Try to have goals that excite you and that mean something. It's easy to get in a rut, so your goals and dreams are a way of escaping that rut. If you are unhappy where you are, then the sensible thing to do is to move. Find new goals, find new directions.

This is your life NOW. Live it now. Don't live it like it will be better in the future. Live it like it will be worse in the future. That way you'll suck as much fun out of it as you can now.

Trans-American Journey Analogy

It's hard to get anywhere if you don't know where you're going. And it's hard to get very far unless you think a long, long, way ahead. You know where you're driving to now, and which direction you're going to take. There might be a few detours along the way. Some road closures due to mudslides, rock falls, floods, and wombat crossings; but if you know where you're going, the detours will only be minor inconveniences. And who knows? You often encounter the best scenery and meet the nicest people on the detours.

in summary

1. Get three unrealistic long-term goals (family, health, and career).

2. Get three realistic long-term goals (family, health, and career).

3. Get three realistic short-term goals for family, health, and career.

4. Get (at least) three dreams that represent achieving each of your unrealistic long-term goals.

5. Pick a goal buddy.

6. Go to *www.simplifyinglife.me* and register your goals.

7. Visualize your unrealistic long-term dreams each night as you are falling asleep.

8. Figure out where you want to go and get moving.

Section 3

Attitudes and Actions
(Road Rules)

So, let's orient ourselves. We've tidied up the loose ends at home prior to the journey. That's good, because you don't want to set off on a trip with the nagging feeling you've left the iron on, do you? Getting your house in order is a metaphor for getting your head in order. We've spent a bit of time picking a destination for the journey, a grand destination, not just the corner shop for a carton of milk.

Now we discuss how to behave on the journey. This is about the road rules, if you like, the ways you should treat others on the trip, how you should you treat yourself, and how you can enjoy the scenery more.

Let's begin. Here are the road rules for your life:

3.1 Pick Good Travelling Companions

I've got this patient I've treated for years. To protect her identity, let's just refer to her as "Misery Guts." Now, I'm a positive guy. I try to cheer people up if they're a little down or a little negative. Misery Guts, however, is beyond cheering up. Her glass isn't just half full; it has a crack in it, and she's sure she's going to knock it over and spill stuff on her new carpet, which is going to stain the carpet because it always stains, and she won't be able to find all the glass, so she'll likely cut her foot later, and it'll get infected, and she'll have to go to hospital, and she'll probably catch a super bug while she's there, and die. Or worse.

Ever met anyone like that? How does that person make you feel?

Possibly the most important part of any journey is choosing who to share it with. An arduous journey can be thoroughly enjoyable with good company. The same is true for your life.

I've been very lucky. I've got a lot of great friends I've known for a long time. Some of them I see all the time. Some of them I only see infrequently. There's something about old friends that's difficult to define. When you share so much history, there is an understanding, a level of communication you don't have with new friends. Old friends are irreplaceable. Don't get me wrong; I value my new friends, too, and hopefully they will become old friends.

I'm also very lucky to have a fantastic wife. She is also an old friend now. She can make me laugh like no one else can, and I love her very much. She is a wonderful and supportive partner on my journey.

Unfortunately, many people grow up with distorted friendship experiences. We're not born with friends. Growing up, you need to learn how to make friendships, and that process is not always easy. You know what I'm talking about. You want to be friends with some other kids, but for whatever reason they manipulate you for their own ends. They make you prove that you're their friend by handing over your lunch money or some other test of loyalty. On one level, they could be insecure and require you to prove yourself to make them feel better. On another level, they may just be bullies exploiting your good intentions.

It can be challenging to know which companions are appropriate for your journey. I find myself less tolerant of negative people these days. I only have to put up with Misery Guts for short periods of time. I have no idea how her friends put up with her. Maybe they're just as negative as she is.

Think about your own circle of friends. How do you feel when you're with positive people, the ones who love knowing what you're doing, the ones who are supportive of your actions, your goals, and your dreams? How does it feel to be with those people? Do you enjoy talking to them? Contrast that with your negative friends, the ones who can see fault with whatever you're doing, the ones who think everything is going to be a problem. How does it feel being with them? Do you look forward to your time together?

Negative people can sap your energy like a bad case of the flu. If you have negative friends who don't support and encourage you, I'd suggest that you consider what your life would be like without them. I know that sounds a little harsh, but do you really need people in your life bringing you down?

As you start your journey through life, the people in your family will be your most important companions. As you grow older you'll start acquiring friends for your journey, and then at some point, if you're lucky, you will find a life partner to sit beside you in the front seat, helping you read the map and suggesting detours. The relative importance of these travelling companions will change as the journey progresses. That's normal. Life is about change, and part of the fun of it is how we deal with those changes.

Pets also make good travelling companions. I don't think you can get enough love in your life, and cats and dogs are great at supplying unconditional love. I'm not sure if a pet bird or snake would be as effective, but if you're sure your snake loves you then don't let me tell you any different. I think pets are particularly important for older people who may have lost a life partner, or people who are lonely for whatever reason. If you think something is missing in your life get a couple of Burmese kittens. Hell, get a couple anyway. We did, and they bring hours of enjoyment. If you're a person who doesn't get a lift out of petting a kitten or a puppy, then nothing I say is going to help you. Go get a snake and see if that works. Keep it away from the kittens though.

Trans-American Journey Analogy

Make sure you have good travelling companions in the car.

→ in summary

> Do you have "friends" who don't have your best interests at heart, people who obstruct your journey? Would you be better off interacting with them less?

3.2 Compliment or Encourage One Person a Day

So, you've chosen who you want in the car with you for the trip, and they're great people. You're sure this trip is going to be a hoot. (Does anyone say that anymore? I guess I just did; so, yes.) Now what? How can you make the trip more satisfying?

I'm forever pondering what would make the world a better place, and I think I have the answer. I probably should come clean first. I don't just care about you; I care about everyone else, too. Now, I appreciate that you're my loyal reader, and I'm doing my darnedest to make your life better, but I've got bigger things in mind. You see, I'm stretching to reach an unrealistic goal just like I told you to do in the last chapter. I want a better life for people who haven't read my book. And this is where you can help me, and help yourself at the same time.

This is a very simple and important rule for living. In fact, I'll go so far as to say it's THE most important rule for living. OK, here it is. Read carefully and slowly.

NEVER let a positive thought
go unexpressed!

I said it was simple, but just ponder that thought for a while. What good does it do you, or anyone else, to keep a positive thought secret? How stupid is that? If you have good news, share it. People love to be complimented. If humans had a happiness meter built into their foreheads, you would see it rise dramatically every time they heard something good said about themselves. You probably think good things about people all the time, but you maybe don't make that small effort to verbalize it. Why is that? Embarrassment? Who knows, but it's about to change.

I want you to start out small. I want you to compliment or encourage ONLY one person a day. I don't care if you have to force yourself to do it, but say something positive to one person. And don't make it some sort of lame cliché like "good job" or "nice work." That doesn't count. The compliment should require you to speak at least an entire sentence.

A good thought about someone locked away in your head does no one any good. Set it free to work its magic. If you tell that someone what your good thought is, they'll feel good, and you'll feel good because they feel good. And they will feel even better because you obviously feel good about them feeling good about what you said. Can you see where this is going? It's a fantastic, positive-feedback loop. And all it takes is for you to open your mouth and verbalize something positive that you're already thinking anyway.

This is my vision. Stick with me because I think it's a good one, and it's my best shot at getting a Nobel Peace Prize. Imagine that you could measure the happiness of the world the same way you can measure temperature. Now pretend that every second person in the world is thinking something positive about the next guy and *actually tells them.* BANG. In an instant, the world's happiness meter goes up. Now, I don't think we're going to get world peace straight away, but the world would be a happier place. Yes, I know it's a corny, touchy-feely idea, but it's fun to ponder (and ponder I do).

All big ideas need to start small. And at this moment, your world is only what you can see from where you're sitting right now. So, let's make that world a better place. Is anyone you know nearby? Is there anything good about them? Can you wander over and tell them? Have you been meaning to tell your wife she's a great mother or a great wife? Or tell your kids that you're proud of them. Maybe you're reading this on a bus or a train. Look around. Can you say anything positive to someone nearby? If you can, do it. Say anything positive. It's fun with people you know, but it's even more fun with complete strangers. Can you spot someone reading a self-help book on the train? Say to them, "Excuse me, but I'm always impressed by people who read books that help them better themselves. Congratulations." That's probably a true statement, don't you think? I mean, you're reading a self-help book, so you must think it's a good idea. This person is probably going to look at you a little strange, but people love compliments, and they feel good when they get them, so I doubt anyone is going to be offended.

So, I want you to start off small and force yourself to do this once a day. Soon you'll be doing it automatically. Eventually, I want you to be able to verbalize every positive thought you have about everyone you interact with.

A related concept is encouragement. Encouragement is similar to a compliment, but different. Whereas a compliment is a pat on the back, encouragement is a pat on the back with a little push. You know what I'm talking about, one of those "go out there and get them" pushes. Never underestimate the power of encouragement. Never. Do I need to repeat that? Let me rephrase it then: Never, ever, ever, (ever) underestimate the power of encouragement. I would never have finished this book without encouragement. I wavered and stalled many times, but each time someone said or did something that kept me going. I remain eternally grateful to those people.

A variation of encouragement is being able to express your expectations for others. Your expectations can change them. If you expect someone to be better, they will be. It's a fascinating way of bending the universe to your will. Try it the next time you get a chance. Pick a candidate, look them in the eye, and say, "I'm expecting great things from you, Craig." (I know a couple of Craigs and I expect great things from them, so pay attention you guys.) I guarantee that if you express high expectations to someone they will remember your words forever and endeavor to be the person you want them to be.

People believe what you tell them. They will embrace the good things and worry about the bad things. Have you ever felt great and then someone says, "You don't look well."? Immediately you don't feel so good. That is the power of suggestion. You can use it for good, not evil, by encouraging someone instead of criticizing them.

One day, a patient (Vic) told me I was a perfectionist. I was focused on other things at the time, but when he planted that positive seed in my head it had no option but to grow. I tried to become what he was encouraging me to become. His words, spoken many years ago, haunt me (in a good way) to this day. You too can give that gift to someone. A few positive words to the right person at the right time can change the world. How awesome is that?

The opposite is also true, so be very careful. If you expect nothing of someone, or the worst of someone, that is also likely to become true. People will become what you expect them to be. It's an invisible force like gravity. Your expectations can lift a person up, or push them down.

Words can be very powerful. People can achieve whatever they believe (that was chapter 2, remember?). People believe good things, or at least want to believe good things about themselves. They're starving for compliments and encouragement. If you encourage someone you could be the little push that makes all the difference, and that can change a life.

Have you heard the theory about the butterfly flapping its wings in the Amazon causing the hurricane in the US? The theory is that little changes can have big consequences, good and bad.

Let me give you an example. A small boy drops his toy as the father is parking the car. The father normally closes the car window after parking, but is distracted by the child. That night a large spider gets into the car and descends on the father the next day as he is driving to work. He panics, loses control of the car, mounts the sidewalk, and badly damages the car. He could have killed himself or a bunch of unsuspecting pedestrians. Do you get my point? Something little can have a knock-on effect that is wildly out of proportion to the original incident.

We have a legendary family story that (I like to think) illustrates this point. I grew up on a farm in the Outback of Australia and went to a small country school (Condobolin High), as did my younger sister, Kerry. In the mid-1980s, Kerry and one of her school friends spent a couple of years travelling through Europe. As luck would have it, her friend's father was a senior executive for News Corporation. The friend's father opened the door for them to work at the company when they would periodically return to London. They'd make some money and then continue travelling.

The father (let's call him John because I've forgotten his name) used to entertain all the time and my sister got to meet a lot of his friends. One day, Kerry was walking down one of the company's corridors when she spotted someone she recognized. Assuming it was one of John's friends she had met before, she pinned him down for a chat. (Country people are like that.) After a polite conversation, my sister returned to her office, which was now in a state of pandemonium. Concerned, she asked what was wrong and found out that Rupert Murdoch was in the building.

Now, in those days Rupert was feared (nothing much has changed) and lots of people were losing their jobs due to restructuring; so, having him turn up often meant a few hundred people would probably be fired.

Then it dawned on my sister: "Ah, that's who I was talking to in the corridor." Kerry hadn't met Rupert before, but she recognized him. Thinking he was one of John's friends, she just decided the polite thing to do was to stop and say hello. I'm confident that not many News Corporation employees in those days were in the habit of cornering Rupert Murdoch for random friendly conversations. My sister, incidentally, said he was very nice.

I like to think that event somehow softened his stance, that somehow a refreshing conversation with a country girl made him want to fire fewer people, that the Condobolin butterfly in London somehow changed the world.

Little seeds grow into big trees, so I want you out there planting lots of seeds. If you have the opportunity to encourage someone, do it. Plant a seed that he or she is destined for greatness, that they will achieve great things. If they already believe that, your encouragement could be all they need to take the next step to greatness. People want to believe in themselves, but when they think other people believe in them, too—wow, that's powerful stuff.

I'm forever telling my two daughters how smart and clever and pretty they are. You can't spend enough time encouraging your kids. They believe everything you tell them, so use that fact to propel them into the future. I try as best I can not to give them any negative thoughts or vibes, particularly seeing as I expect them to write a book about how wonderful a father I am. If you're in the habit of criticizing your kids (maybe because your parents did it to you), then get out of the habit.

Compliment or encourage? I don't care which you choose. It's all fruit from the same tree, it's all good, it's all positive. It is a wonderful gift to be able to make another human being feel better with just a few words. I discussed my book ideas with friends many times, and without their encouragement I probably wouldn't have finished it. And if I hadn't finished it I wouldn't have the opportunity to encourage you to encourage others. That butterfly certainly gets around. Never underestimate your ability to make a difference in the world with just a few words.

Trans-American Journey Analogy

There's no road rage on your journey. You wait for little old ladies to cross the road, you help stranded motorists, you make room for people to change lanes, and you smile at other people stopped at traffic lights.

in summary

Verbalize every positive thought you have about another person TO THEM. Your greatest ability is the power to encourage someone else to reach their full potential. It is a wonderful and free gift, so give freely.

3.3 Start Writing "Lifeogies"

Yes, Lifeogy (pronounced life-o-gee) is a made-up word, but it sums up perfectly how you can take my "sharing positive thoughts" idea to the next level. I'm eternally grateful to my goal buddy and coach Ronan Lutman for coining the word. It was a stroke of genius.

Let me share my thinking process here. I have a mentor, Dr. Omer Reed (I tell a little of his story later in the book), who has affected me in ways he can't imagine. (He can't imagine yet, but he'll know soon.) Omer is not a young man, and has had some recent health challenges.

I'm a bit of a daydreamer. I like to let my mind wander. Often my thoughts drift in interesting directions and deliver me new ideas (thank you mind). So, I was daydreaming about Omer and his health, and I decided that if he died I'd try to get to the US (I'm in Australia) for his funeral to show his wife Marci what he meant to me. Then I thought I'd like to say a few words at his funeral. Then I started thinking what I would say, and then it hit me: What good is a eulogy to a dead person?

I'm pretty confident that a person's hearing and eyesight decline markedly after death. Bearing that in mind, I think it's absolutely stupid to wait for someone to die before you compose and express your thoughts about what they meant to you. Wouldn't it be smarter to do that before they died? At that point my wandering mind decided that rather than delivering a eulogy at Omer's funeral, I should do a living eulogy so he gets to know how I feel BEFORE he dies.

I discussed this idea with Ronan my goal buddy, and we decided "Living Eulogy" sounded a bit bleak and negative, and that we needed a new word that was more positive. And in a matter of moments the word Lifeogy was born.

My editor shared a story that sums up the power of the process: "Before my wife's mother died (2012), I had all her close friends send me an email with recollections of what they had learned, gained, and enjoyed from being with her. I got about one hundred or more letters. I published them in a book, with some photos, and we gave it to her before she died. Now there is a copy of the book for each family member and the one hundred people who wrote a letter. I like your idea a lot. It's powerful."

How brilliant an idea is that? Wouldn't you just love to read messages about yourself, as opposed to NOT hearing them after you are dead? I would like to formalize the process, however, to make it easy and simple to apply (sounds like something I'd want to do, doesn't it?).

So, here's what I want YOU to do. I want you to make a list of people you would like to write a Lifeogy for. If you struggled with the chapter 1 challenge, then you might want to do one for your parents first. If you have estranged friends or relatives, you could do one for them. It could be an ice breaker.

Write a list now (and I mean NOW). Number the order you want to do them in. It will probably be a list of your closest friends and family members, but it could include other people, too. Teachers, co-workers, neighbors, random celebrities—just about anyone really. If you have strong emotions about a person, you could write him or her a Lifeogy.

But what do I say, Brett? Excellent question. I've been pondering that and I'm going to suggest a formula. Please don't feel you have to follow it; it's just to give you a framework to make it easier. Being honest is what is critical to the process.

My Lifeogy Formula:

1. Explanation

2. First memory

3. Strongest memory

4. Fondest or funniest memory, and the times you have enjoyed together

5. Effect on your life, and what you have learned from the person

6. Attributes

7. Lasting legacy, or what you will always remember about them

Since it was Omer who sparked my thinking in this area, I'm going to do his first as an example for you. Here it is:

Hi Omer,

(Explanation) *I'm writing living eulogies (called Lifeogies) for the people who mean the most to me. Below is yours. I hope you like it.*

(First memory) *I was sort of aware you existed before I knew who you were, or ever met you. My first real memory of you was a lecture you delivered via video to the EPG group. My strong recollection was that your ideas were different and profound. Even from that first impersonal long-distance meeting (where you didn't get to meet me) I knew you were different.*

My next strongest memory of you was when you were sitting in about the fifth row, directly in front of me, during a lecture I gave in Chicago. The room was full of hundreds of people, I was nervous as hell, and there, sitting right in front of me, is one of the legends of the industry. Great! I was nervous enough to start, but having you there made me more nervous. I remember acknowledging your presence, and then weaving that fact into my lecture to make a point which helped my cause immensely. So, that made me a little less nervous, and then my first few jokes went down well, and the lecture seemed to go over OK. So, our first encounter was a positive one.

(Strongest memory) *Then came the moment that changed my life. I was having dinner that night (after the lecture) with Bill and his family. You came up to say hello and offered me your life's work to carry on! To say I was in shock does not do the moment justice. It is one of my strongest memories in life and it haunts me.*

Why does it haunt me? At first I was profoundly honored. That emotion eventually morphed into fear and trepidation at the enormity of the task of doing your life's work justice. And then over the years, this fear morphed into guilt for not following through with propagating your wisdom. It has taken me many years to truly appreciate your gift.

(Effect on your life) *And what was it? It was the gift of confidence, possibly the greatest gift you can give someone. Your faith in me helped me pursue my own path. Yes, I still feel a little bit guilty about the fact that (up until this point) I was not focused on propagating the totality of your message. But I'm doing my best (with my book) to convey some of your wisdom to a larger audience.*

(Attributes) *And what is that wisdom? The importance of thinking for yourself. The importance of thinking differently. The importance of overcoming adversity. The importance of communicating effectively. The importance of being present with people (sadly becoming a lost art). I can never have a conversation with you without later pondering the meaning of your words. I can't think of anyone else who makes me think as deeply as you do.*

(Lasting legacy) *Your words, Omer, and the way you have conducted yourself, will live with me long after you are gone. I'm grateful I have had the opportunity to get to know you (and the gorgeous Marci) over the years, and I'm particularly grateful for your kindness, your confidence, and your support. I have a lot of acquaintances, but few true friends. You, however, are a true friend.*

Sincerely,
Brett

So, I didn't follow the formula exactly. I really haven't spent a lot of time with Omer, so I couldn't think of any funny memories. How you write a Lifeogy is not what's important. You're not trying to win a Pulitzer Prize here. What's important is to put your positive and fond thoughts, feelings, and emotions into words, and to share those words. It's a whole lot more fun sharing your positive emotions with the living than it is with the dead.

Don't make this an onerous project. Take two minutes to write your list and five or ten minutes to write each Lifeogy. I feel very confident the response you will get from your first Lifeogy will inspire you to write more.

Trans-American Journey Analogy

In the old days when people travelled and were a long way from home, the only way you could communicate was with letters. And those letters often contained a lot of positive emotions. Let's pretend, then, that you're in a bygone era, and that you want to put into words what you're thinking about a loved one or friend.

in summary

No one likes speaking at funerals, but that's where you often hear the best stories about people. It makes no sense to wait until someone dies before penning a few words about what they mean to you. The time to do it is before they die. The time to do it is now.

3.4 Do Something for Someone

I love people fussing over me. It makes me feel all warm and fuzzy inside. I even like going to the dentist because I enjoy the attention. (I've got a great dentist, though.) Anyway, the point is, it feels good having things done for you, so turn that around and do things for other people.

It's a simple process. Just look for opportunities to do something for someone. It doesn't have to take a lot of time, but your kindness will brighten someone's day. It works best if it's unexpected, which may be a challenge if you get into a bit of a routine, but you have to start somewhere.

Here are a few examples of things you could do:

1. Make a cup of tea for a coworker.

2. Offer to pick up lunch for a coworker.

3. Ask your boss if there is anything you can do for him/her before you go home.

4. Open doors for people.

5. Do anything unexpected for your spouse. For men, this is easy because they generally do so little. Women may have to think a little harder about the few things they don't already do.

6. OK, number five wasn't very helpful. Men should choose some task normally done by the wife and insist on doing it for her. You could say something like this: "Honey, you sit down and read a book. I'm washing up, loading the dishwasher, making dinner, bathing the kids, and washing and ironing the clothes tonight."

For women, if you can find something (anything) your husband does, then let him off the hook every now and then. (Sorry, I can't get serious about men doing stuff. That probably reflects badly on me.) Women could make a special breakfast for their husbands, maybe a cup of tea and some toast in bed.

This is not supposed to be an elaborate process. It's something I want you doing every day for someone (preferably a different person each day), and it should take no time at all. It's a way of saying, "I'm thinking about you and I like to help." The task is largely irrelevant; it's about the receiver knowing that someone is looking out for them.

Trans-American Journey Analogy

Remember how you felt when the attendant washed your windows at a gas station? You younger people have no idea what I'm talking about, do you? OK, remember how you felt when you let someone merge in front of you and you got the little "thank you" wave? Well, try to do that every day.

→ **in summary**

Kindness is the oil that takes the friction out of life (that's not my line, but I like it). Do something for someone every day. It will make you both feel good.

3.5 One Belly Laugh

I've always loved to laugh. There's something about laughing that is profoundly healthy. I'm sure there's research to support that assertion, but I'm too lazy to look for it. Even if it wasn't good for you (and I'm sure it is), it's a lot of fun. It's hard to have a bad time when you're laughing.

I believe laughing is often a choice. Sure, if something is sad, it would be almost impossible to force out a chuckle. But as a general rule, it isn't hard to find SOMETHING to laugh about each day.

The thing about laughing, and particularly a good belly laugh, is that it clears the cobwebs out of your head. You know how air feels clean after it rains? Well, that's how your head feels after a good laugh. If you're not the laughing type, you need to become the laughing type. I can think of a bunch of sad-sack people who never laugh, and a bunch of happy people who laugh about anything. Same world, different attitudes. So how do you get yourself a humor transplant?

It is possible to laugh even in the absence of anything funny. Try it now. Make yourself laugh. Squeeze out a chuckle for no apparent reason.

Did you do it? You know how cranky I get when people don't do what they're told when they're told. If you didn't do it, do it now. If you've already done it, do it again. Squeeze out a laugh and add a little chuckle at the end. If you're in a place where this is going to be embarrassing, that's even better. Someone might get a laugh watching you laugh.

One of the great things about laughing is that it's infectious, pretty much like yawning is. By the way, did you just yawn when I mentioned yawning? Isn't that weird? I've just yawned three times as I've read back the last sentence. Now it's four times. Anyway, if someone starts laughing, I mean really laughing, the people around them will quickly start to laugh for no reason. It's almost impossible not to. First, you'll smile and say, "What's so funny?" If they keep laughing you'll start to chuckle, and if they're in the middle of one of those fantastic "tears in your eyes," breathless, belly laughs, it's possible you will be swept along to the same level of frenzy without having any idea what was so funny in the first place. And you'll feel great.

I had a fabulous dinner with one of my best friends (Ammie) after a particularly stressful day for both of us (we were drilling each other's teeth for hours). At some point during dinner (there was wine involved), she says something we both found exceptionally funny. Now, I'm a "practice what you preach" sort of guy, so I chose to immerse myself in the moment. It was the most I've laughed in my life. We were breathless and our faces were covered in tears. I honestly almost wet myself. The next day she texted me the punchline to the joke while I was sitting in an airplane during boarding. I laughed so hard that half people in the plane were staring at me. It felt great.

So, let's assume laughing is a choice. You can squeeze out some sort of laugh on demand without anything being funny (go ahead, do it again) and you can laugh along with someone when you don't know what they're laughing about. Squeezing out a laugh isn't very satisfying unless you're with a bunch of people doing the same thing, in which case you might end up in one of those infectious, belly laugh situations. If you have enough time, organize a laughing club. For the rest of you I have another plan.

I want you to make yourself laugh when something is even mildly amusing. You have a choice. You can read or hear something funny and choose to suppress a laugh, or you can choose to let one go. I'm suggesting you start choosing to let one rip. (That was a fart gag. Are you laughing?) It really isn't that hard once you practice a little. Choose to find things funny. Choose to laugh about those things and exaggerate the laugh when you do. Force any laugh as far as it will go. Try it for the rest of the book. I'm sure I will say something mildly amusing in the next hundred or so pages. Just laugh at my poor sentence construction if nothing else grabs you.

So mobilize the giggle gear, people. Start choosing to find everything as funny as possible and really blow the cobwebs out of your mind.

Trans-American Journey Analogy

Make a decision to find bumper stickers funnier than they actually are and laugh out loud. Look out the window of your car and see the world as a fun place and try to make it a little more fun.

→ in summary

Force yourself to have at least one belly laugh a day. It's easy once you get the hang of it, and a LOT of fun.

3.6 Exultation

I've had more than my fair share of ups and downs. I alluded to the fact earlier that I'd "died" a couple of times. I did that for dramatic effect. What I meant was that my heart has been stopped a couple of times. Prior to my "character building" cancer, I had open heart surgery twice (at ages twenty-three and forty-six). I was born with a couple of heart defects that required a bit of plumbing revision. If you've never had your chest cut open, good for you. It's something best avoided, but as I keep telling you, I like to learn from everything.

So, what have I learned? Well, life has lots of highs and lows. It's unavoidable, so get used to it. The down times make you appreciate the up times more. You need both. Everything is relative.

You can't enjoy your life if all you do is enjoy your life. You need the contrast. Suppose you had unlimited wealth and unlimited time to enjoy it. How much would you enjoy it? You're probably thinking, "I could take a pretty good shot at enjoying it, Brett," and I'm sure you would for a while. But without contrast it wouldn't stay enjoyable forever, or at least not at the same level.

Suppose you love chocolate, but you only get to have one small piece once a week. That one small piece of chocolate a week tastes fantastic. But what if you get one piece a day, or one piece an hour, or one piece a minute? If you eat chocolate all day, will each piece taste as good as it did when you could only have one piece a week? Of course not. Do a test if you don't believe me (buy some larger pants before you start).

It's all relative. If you work five long days a week, then Friday night is special. If you don't work, then Friday night is just like any other night. If you only have two weeks of vacation a year, those times are special. If you were permanently on holidays, would each week be special? I'm not saying you can't enjoy yourself, but it's the contrast that makes it special. Two people can have the same experience (say a week's holiday in Fiji) and perceive it differently. If it is your only holiday for the year and you've never been to Fiji, you'll probably have a great time (like I did when I went). If you've been ten times before and you're in the middle of a year's holiday you probably won't have as much fun. Same holiday, just viewed from two different perspectives.

Most of us get into ruts sometimes. Things seem the same. No highs, no lows. One way to steer yourself out of a rut is with exultation. By that I mean finding things that will predictably bring you exultation, something that lifts your spirits, something that picks you up, excites you, snaps you out of the malaise, and gets your pulse racing.

You need to find what works for you, but for me it's music. If I feel I'm in a funk I play one of my favorite songs loud. I leave a CD of my favorite songs in the car. Generally, I play at least one of them on the way to work and on the way home. It always picks me up. Remember the relativity rule, though. If you play your favorite song a hundred times a day it won't be your favorite song for long, so mix them up.

Sport can be another way to bring exultation into your life. There's nothing better than watching your favorite team win. Of course, if they get soundly beaten each week, it's not going to work. But if you can be pragmatic about a few losses, you should be able to get some exultation out of the losses.

TV shows and movies can be another way to lift your spirits. My wife and I are *Star Trek* fans. We don't dress up or anything (not in *Star Trek* costumes anyway, but that's a different story). We've watched almost all of the TV series and enjoyed it greatly. Now, years later, we're watching the episodes again on DVD. We know we're going to enjoy them and it gives us that little lift. Watching new episodes of our favorite TV shows does the same thing.

Religion can be a source of exultation. I'm going to discuss spirituality at the end of the book, but if hearing a good sermon picks you up, then get out there and be picked up.

Whatever works for you, start incorporating that into your life on a regular basis. Think about the things that pick you up, excite you, and send tingles down your spine. Then inject them into your life more frequently. Don't make it haphazard, plan the excitement. Have them available in case of emergency. These days I always have my favorite songs ready in a play list on my phone in case I need them.

So, like everything else, let's do our homework now so we don't get distracted. We are so easily distracted these days, aren't we? These are a few things that bring me exultation:

1. My favorite songs played loud

2. Going fast in my boat (when it's safe, of course)

3. Taking the roof off my car on a sunny day

4. Watching my favorite TV shows

Now it's your turn. Write four things down that "pick you up":

1. _____

2. _____

3. _____

4. _____

Trans-American Journey Analogy

You've been driving for hours and your favorite song of all time comes on the radio. It's the one you've never been able to get a copy of. (I know that doesn't happen these days, but just pretend.) How do you feel? Well, recreate that feeling as often as possible.

→ in summary

Find things that lift your spirits and be lifted regularly.

3.7 Anticipation

I vividly recall lying in an uncomfortable hospital bed after my last heart operation. I was visualizing myself waking up in my own comfortable bed, sun shining on my face, looking out the window at the trees, and the light twinkling on the river. The thought of that moment brought me great joy.

Life is not all beer and skittles. We can't do fun things all day long, and if we did they wouldn't seem fun anymore. (Read the contrast principle in the last section.) A lot in your life is going to be bland or boring. You might not be lucky enough to love your job. Plenty of people need to work in jobs that don't thrill them. That's life, which is why it is important to ALWAYS have something to look forward to, something in the future that keeps you going.

Most working people anticipate the weekend, or anticipate their free time. I don't want you to obsess about how great your weekend will be, or how crappy the rest of your working week is. That isn't healthy. But it is normal to look forward to going home, weekends, etc.

Planning a vacation can bring immense satisfaction. Many people derive as much joy out of the planning as they do out of the actual trip. That's the beauty of anticipation.

The point is, it's important to have things to look forward to. You should always have something you are anticipating, some beacon of hope and enjoyment in the distance that helps drag you through the less-fun bits of your life. Don't only focus on the beacon. Remember, life is a journey, not a destination; but a little anticipation is healthy. Using the journey analogy, anticipation is where you stop for lunch. It's a rest break in life.

Things you might anticipate other than holidays are:

1. Concerts by your favorite performers (these are often booked months in advance)

2. Sporting events

3. Regular boys' night or girls' night out

4. Dinners with friends

5. Birthday and anniversary dinners

This is what I'm anticipating at the moment:

1. Bushwalking in Tasmania with my wife and friends after Christmas

2. A weekend family holiday by the beach

3. A Bruce Springsteen concert (I have tickets!)

4. Getting the book finished (it's an obsession at the moment)

What are you looking forward to? You know the rules. Write them down:

1. _____

2. _____

3. _____

Trans-American Journey Analogy

There's nothing better on a long trip than knowing you're going to stop for an hour or two at your favorite hamburger joint.

→ **in summary**

Always have some event planned that you can anticipate with excitement.

3.8 Traditions and Rituals

My wife and I (and now our kids) have dinner every Sunday night with a group of friends at the same Chinese restaurant. We've been doing that for over twenty-five years. We catch up on the week, exchange stories, discuss issues, tell jokes, talk nonsense, gossip, give advice, whatever. We've watched our kids grow up. We've watched our hair fall out, our bellies get bigger, our careers change, our parents get old, our families move away. Before we know it, our kids will move away and, sadly, one day our parents will die.

Different friends and family make guest appearances but the core people (Dave, Karen, Blake, Brett, Donna, Lauren, Sophie) are there pretty much every week. It is a wonderful constant that I cherish and look forward to every Sunday.

It's reassuring to have constants in your life. By constants, I mean familiar, reoccurring, and regular activities like birthdays, anniversaries, Christmas, etc. If you don't like those things, keep reading this book until you do, or buy the hardcover version and bang your head with it because you should look forward to those things. The only reason lots of people find Christmas stressful is because they have unresolved family issues, and they're forced to confront family at Christmas. If your family still scares you, then you didn't nail chapter 1, did you?

Where was I? Oh yeah, tradition and ritual. Familiarity can be very comforting. Patterns that underpin your life can be a foundation around which to live the rest of your life. It doesn't matter how crazy things get, rituals and traditions shared with family and friends can be a haven, a safe place you can depend on to escape from whatever is bothering you. Rituals and tradition can almost anchor your life.

My Sunday-night dinner with friends and family is something I've been able to look forward to every week for more than twenty-five years. It's a little piece of joy I can depend on. That is the power of rituals and traditions. (I don't know if this is a ritual or a tradition, so I'm lumping the two concepts together.)

So, if you don't have any already, I want you to get your own rituals and traditions. You have to start somewhere, so just start. Try to make it a constant, not just some loose agreement to meet. Lots of people regularly have dinner with their parents. I think that's great. My parents have only recently moved closer to us, so they're now part of the Sunday-night crowd.

Do you have any close friends? Get something constant happening. It doesn't have to be once a week. Once a month is fine, but you should have something regular to anticipate. My Sunday-night dinner friends, Dave and Karen, have another ritual I'm a part of. They host a seafood BBQ every Good Friday. That tradition has been going on for over thirty years. Their old friends from school (who are mostly my old friends from school) turn up. I only see a lot of these people once a year. It's a fabulous day and a great way to keep in touch and reminisce about the old days with people you would otherwise drift away from. I'm not a great one for reminiscing. I think you should live in the present and look forward to the future, but a little reminiscing once a year is OK.

Another ritual I had for many years was visiting my grandmother with my two daughters every Saturday morning. The kids and I would have breakfast at the local deli on our way there. Back in my carnivore days (more on that later), I'd have a bacon and egg roll and a cappuccino. I used to love bacon and egg rolls, and I'd only ever allow myself one a week, so Saturday breakfasts were special. Little Sophie got her chocolate milkshake, which she only spilled every third Saturday. We'd finish our breakfast and go to visit Granny. We did that right up until she died at age ninety-eight. It might seem boring and mundane to you, but for me it was something enjoyable that I could rely on each week.

Good friends of ours have a fantastic tradition that I intend to steal. They have three daughters (we have two) and the father decided he wanted to do a father-daughter bonding thing when they started high school. Each of his daughters got to pick a destination somewhere in the world, and that's where dad and daughter went. I thought it was just a fiendish ruse to get away on a ski trip without the missus. As it turned out the first daughter wanted to go skiing, but the second one wanted to go to Disneyland, so he struck out there. Actually, he told me it was a fantastic experience and he spent quality time with each of them (and did a little skiing, too).

Now his wife has retaliated. She instituted her own tradition, which is to take each of the girls away for their sixteenth birthday. The first trip was to Paris. What a great idea. I'm going to do it myself, provided my girls like skiing.

So, get yourself some rituals or start a few traditions. I suggest you start with one involving family and one involving friends. Decide on a frequency you can commit to (weekly or monthly) and stick to it. If it's not working, or you don't look forward to it, or it's not fun, get another one. This is not supposed to be a chore. It is a fun and reassuring constant you that you can insert into your life. Put your thinking cap on and write down your rituals:

1. Family ritual:_____

2. Friend ritual:_____

Trans-American Journey Analogy

There are a bunch of lookouts I never pass. I've seen the views one hundred times, but I still enjoy them.

→ in summary

Looking forward to regular, pleasurable events can be a reassuring and fun constant in your life. Start a regular family and friend ritual that will one day become a tradition.

3.9 Be Happy Where You Are (Enjoy the Journey)

Most of this book is simple. You've probably figured that out already (hell, it's not a secret; it's written on the cover). Simple ideas, however, are easy to overlook in a complex world, a world driven by clever marketers whose very existence depends on us being dissatisfied with life. How can they make a living if you remain satisfied with your old car, your small TV, your last-season's clothes, and your unfashionable mobile phone? There is an entire industry out there devoted to making you feel like there's something missing in your life.

Now I'm the last person to suggest you shouldn't wander down the mall and oil the wheels of commerce with your hard-earned cash. Buy a few more copies of my book for your friends while you're down there. There's nothing wrong with buying things, provided you can afford them. But remember this important fact: Buying things won't make you happy.

If you're not happy where you are, you're not going to be happier somewhere else. If you're not happy with the things you have, you aren't going to be any happier with different things.

Read that last paragraph again. It will save you a lot of money and a lot of grief. Things don't make you happy. If they did, you wouldn't have to get rid of them to buy new things. If that new car was going to make you happy, you'd keep it for twenty years. How many people keep cars for twenty years?

It's a trap to believe that happiness and contentment are out there in the future. So many people get stuck in a cycle of thinking they'll be happy when they retire, or when they get a raise, or when they get a bigger house, or when they get a new car. But you know what? If those things do make you a little happier, it won't last for long.

You know the saying: "The grass is always greener on the other side of the fence." Well, the better place is often an illusion. Once you get on the other side of the fence it starts to look pretty good where you were.

Work on being happy where you are before you concentrate on getting somewhere else, because it is likely you won't be any happier there.

Happiness is all about choice. It's all about choosing your own reality. If you think you're happy, then you are happy. No discussion no argument. The same goes for negative emotions (fear, unhappiness, uncertainty). You choose your reality. In almost all circumstances a positive spin can be found.

I was attending a conference in the US when my rental car got towed away. Everyone was expecting me to be upset but it was the highlight of the trip. A good mate (Mark) drove me around that evening to pick up things I needed, so I got to spend some time with him and his wife. The next day another good mate (Bill) drove me to the repo yard to fetch the car. He had his kids with him, and we all got to have an interesting adventure. (Those repo yards are another world.) Anyway, I had some great experiences with some great friends that wouldn't have occurred if my car hadn't been towed. As I mentioned before, you can meet the nicest people and have some of the most interesting experiences when life throws you a curveball.

It's all about perception, it's all about attitude, and it's all about choice. No one can MAKE you unhappy, only YOU can make you unhappy, which is great because it means the opposite is also true. If you want to be happy just choose to be happy. Look at the Dalai Lama. He ALWAYS looks happy, doesn't he? His country has been stolen and his people have been persecuted, but he's still always happy. What right do you have to be unhappy?

This process of choosing happiness is a lot easier if all of your ducks are in a row (if you finish reading the book and adopt a few of the ideas), but even if you do nothing I suggest, you can still be profoundly happy if you choose that for yourself.

People are so obsessed with getting places, with achieving things, with attaining things, and with completing tasks that they often ignore the fact that getting there is generally more fun than being there (with the possible exception of cramped bus, train, and airline travel—where one's knees are too proximal to one's nose).

My late uncle, Ron Taylor, was successful and well-known in Australia. He was a marine conservationist and shark expert who filmed some of the footage for the movie *Jaws*. Many years ago, he told me that the most fun he ever had in life was struggling to achieve his dream. The bit he enjoyed was the struggling, not the achieving. Once you get to the top there are lots of pressures, but when you're figuring out how to get there you have the most fun. I'm not sure if struggling is fun if you never achieve the dream. But the reality is that you HAVE to enjoy the journey because most of your life is going to be the journey. The journey IS your life. I'll say it again: The journey is your life.

It's tempting to think a different part of the journey will be easier or more satisfying. Maybe it will be, maybe it won't. Your life, however, is NOW. So, I hope you follow up on what's in this book and make your life simpler and happier, but I'm not telling you to get a different job, wife, house, or life. Whatever you have now is what I want you to work with. You can have a great time now, wherever you happen to be on your journey.

Nicole Kidman said (and I paraphrase), "The simple things in life are better than the grand things. I've experienced both and the simple is better." You can be happy with anything. Don't be fooled by the incorrect perception that grand things, or any things for that matter, will make you happier. Don't live life expecting to win a lottery, because even if you do win, you'll realize that you're still you when the dust settles, only now with a little more time on your hands (which may be a bad thing). Get to like YOU, get to be happy with YOU and your life regardless of your circumstances. The grass may look greener over the fence, but it isn't. You can be happy with anything or unhappy with anything. The choice is yours.

Trans-American Journey Analogy

If you look at the faces of your fellow travelers, you will notice their apparent happiness is in no way related to the cost of their cars. The more expensive the car, the more grim-faced the driver. Maybe they're stressing about the insurance premiums.

→ in summary

If you're not happy where you are or with what you have, don't fool yourself into thinking you'll be any happier somewhere else. You can choose to be happy with your life as it is. Don't be fooled into thinking you'll be happier when . . .

3.10 Be Open to Serendipity and Synchronicity

I've always felt I was lucky, and that is the perception others have of me. It's no accident. My father told me I was lucky when I was young and I believed him; consequently, I've always expected good things to happen to me. So, what I do is project this idea that I'm lucky into the universe. I visualize myself being lucky. I visualize good things happening to me. I visualize things I want to happen. If I'm driving somewhere, I visualize where I want to park when I get there. More often than not, I get a parking spot where I want it; not always, but enough that people notice my "ability."

When I was younger, I used to visualize myself accidentally meeting girls I was interested in. Once, when I was about thirteen, I did that in the morning, caught two buses, and "accidentally" bumped into a girl I was interested in—at a place I couldn't have guessed she'd be. Very spooky and very cool (for a thirteen-year-old). Pity I didn't visualize her going out with me.

I'm not sure that we fully understand how electricity works, but it does. Not knowing how it works doesn't mean the lights aren't going to come on tonight when you hit the switch. The same goes for gravity. That isn't fully understood either, but the earth isn't about to fling itself into the cosmos just because we don't understand what keeps it where it is. And then there's Dark Matter. They say 84.5 percent of the mass of the universe is made up of something we've never seen, and don't really understand.

My point is that just because you don't understand something doesn't mean it doesn't exist or it isn't true.

There's a fine line between skepticism and stupidity. As a dentist, I'm a man of science, so I don't lap up every idiot idea out there. But I also think it's very arrogant to assume we know it all, or about what "all" is, or anything at "all" compared to what there is to know. Let's get things in perspective: We've only been able to fly for the last one hundred-ish years. It's only been fifty-odd years since we fired something into space. We've really done nothing grand, cosmically speaking. We're very proud of our achievements and knowledge, but relative to what? Ourselves? Big deal.

I am flabbergasted by the arrogance of people who assume that because something isn't proven, it will never be proven. Evidence does not define or display truth, it merely determines the current level of ignorance. Knowledge moves on. You can't be certain something is "true." Things just appear to be true given the available knowledge that can, in the fullness of time, be superseded. I know a few things I think are true, but there are very few things I know for certain are untrue. Ponder that a while. I've got a lot of theories, but that is probably my favorite.

So, what's all this got to do with serendipity and synchronicity? Serendipity means "making fortunate discoveries by accident." I just don't believe the discoveries are an accident. Carl Jung, the philosopher, introduced the concept of synchronicity, which he said is "the experience of having two (or more) things happen coincidentally in a manner that is meaningful to the person or persons experiencing them." Again, I don't think it's coincidence.

I recently had a fascinating example of synchronicity. I'd come up with an interesting analogy for chapter 6 one morning. That afternoon I was treating a patient I'd known for many years, and for some reason I wanted to mention my idea to him. Up until that point, I had only told one or two of my patients that I was writing a book. So, get this image in your head. Julian (my patient) is lying there with his mouth wide open and full of hardware and spit. I like to talk to my patients to distract them from what I'm doing, so they're used to me chatting. I briefly told Julian that I was writing a book and I told him about my chapter 6 idea. At that point, I thought he was going to choke, that something went down his throat. But after I disentangled him from all the paraphernalia, it turned out that Julian had written three chapters of his own book on exactly the topic I was discussing (an esoteric religious theory). How spooky is that? I don't have a dental practice filled with patients who write esoteric religious novels. You'd be hard pressed to find more than a handful of my patients who are regular church-goers (I think my sense of humor keeps the pious types away), and Julian just happened to turn up on the day I'd written something about a topic that interested him. I just happened to mention it to him even though I hadn't mentioned it to anyone else (before or since). If that isn't synchronicity, I don't know what is. Julian gave me an idea for a slightly different approach to chapter 6, which you can read when you get there. I'm grateful to him and the synchronicity fairies for the input and the meeting.

So, this is what I think: There's something going on. Call it fate, call it karma, call it God, call it intuition, call it synchronicity, call it destiny, call it anything you want; but I've noticed forces in life that I can't explain. I don't think life is random. I think there is something that gently propels or guides us through life. I imagine we are all connected by fine threads, like spider webs, and that all these webs are connected to each other and to something else. I have no idea what that something is. The link is not strong. It's a very fine connection that is easily ignored, but it can be noticed if you choose to. We are pulled in different directions, but we can also pull on the web ourselves. Yes, it seems like voodoo, but if you open your eyes to it, you will be amazed what you notice. What is this force, this connection? I have no idea, and I'm never going to know, but that doesn't bother me. If you want to think it's God guiding your life, then go with that. If you think it's destiny predetermined by some universal force, then go with that. I sort of think it's God and I sort of think it's destiny and I sort of think it's some other force. Like I said before, just because you don't understand something doesn't mean it doesn't exist.

So how do I use this force? Well, yes, I do use it to find parking spaces. Apart from that I just try to be aware that it's there. I try not to ignore all the messages that life is trying to give me. That's often hard when you lead a busy life, but I try when possible to be attuned. I don't think coincidences are coincidences, I always assume there's some reason behind them, and I endeavor to seek out that reason. I assume life is trying to guide me and I allow myself to be guided.

You need to have an underlying assumption that good things are going to happen to you (which IS my underlying assumption), and that there is a reason to life (I believe that, too). I also believe you need a lot of trust. That seems to work. I sort of believe in God, but I don't believe in religion (more of that in chapter 6). If you believe in God, it's easy to think it's HIS will guiding you, and I don't have a problem with that. I don't think you need to be a believer to use this force though. Believers think God has a purpose for them and maybe the universe has a purpose in mind for all of us, or maybe it doesn't. We certainly have enough free will to ignore the force. If you buy into the idea of karma, and you bite the guiding hand, you may end up in a place you don't really like.

I'm not constantly using my will to pull on the spider webs; mostly, I'm just paying attention to the force without trying to affect it. Now that I think about it, it's very much a *Star Wars* philosophy. Actually, now that I really think about it, it's exactly like the concept of the force in *Star Wars,* except I think it's real, not fiction. (Maybe George Lucas thinks it's real, too; I'd like to ask him sometime.)

Let me be clear: I'm talking about listening to the good voices, not the bad ones. If you're hearing voices telling you to burn something, don't listen to those. Do no evil. If you hear a voice that wants you to do something that impacts anyone negatively, then that's not the voice I want you listening to. I'm talking about that little voice that turns up every now and then and tries to guide you. Life sends out lots of messages and the better you are able to listen, the better off you will be. Don't ignore them. Maybe I'm one of those little voices while you're reading the book. Who knows?

I heard a guy called W. Mitchell speak at a conference I attended a few years ago. He has been severely injured twice and now he gives a motivating talk about overcoming adversity. He said that before his second accident (a plane crash) he experienced a very strong sense of impending doom. He had a premonition of what was going to happen; however, he ignored it. He makes the point, and I'm paraphrasing, that, "Someone tried to kill me twice to get my attention, so now I'm listening."

This book was almost finished ten years ago. After a lot of hard work and many rejections I found a literary agent who thought she could get it published. Unfortunately, she got sick and had to let me go, which took the wind out of my sails for a long time.

Then I got cancer in my neck.

To be completely honest, I'm finishing the book because after two open-heart operations and getting cancer, I'm more than a little worried someone is trying to kill me to get my attention. So now I'm listening.

Here's what I've learned. If you ever get the feeling someone is trying to tell you something, then they probably are. If you keep bumping into the same stranger, then strike up a conversation. That person may have something to tell you. Life is gently trying to push us all in a certain direction. My experience is that the direction is good. Go with the flow. Keep an open mind but don't be gullible.

I'm convinced that life conspired against me to get this book written. Lots of obstacles were put in my way to make sure I took the correct path and learned the correct lessons. If you find your life is being guided, go with it and don't fight against it.

One word of caution, however. Don't let yourself be paralyzed by the process. Don't over-think everything you do. It's easy to convince yourself that every plane you board is about to fall out of the sky (if you're a nervous flyer). The idea is not to become paranoid.

So, this is what I want you to do: Be aware. That's all, just be aware that life may be trying to teach you something or tell you something. Treat all coincidences as messages. Imagine there are little forces dragging you in certain directions and allow yourself to be dragged. Don't ignore intuition. If you've got a feeling about something, go with it and explore it. If you want to take it to the next level like me, then try bending the universe to your will. Visualize good things happening.

Use the force, Luke (or whatever your name is).

Postscript

It's hard to be honest writing a book. It seems (to the reader) like it's written in one long sequential session, but that ain't the case. It gets written, rewritten, chopped, changed, and then edited over a long time. So, there you have it. Now you know the truth. Some of the words you've read so far were written fifteen-years ago. Some were written more recently (like this postscript).

At the moment, I'm on holiday at a beachside town with my wife and daughters, making final revisions based on my editor's suggestions.

I'm getting up early to work so I don't steal time from the family. I've just revised the serendipity section above and gone out for a coffee. I'm walking back with my coffee and I have this strong desire to approach a group of cyclists. It felt a bit awkward, but my own words are ringing in my ears, so I stop and talk to them. I've been after a mountain bike to rent, and they happen to know (because they're longtime locals) a guy who does specialist bike rentals and private tours. I ring him up and he's got a great bike to rent and he's going out for a ride with some mates that afternoon and he offers to take me out. I researched this trip for six months and never found this guy online, but one quick serendipitous conversation transforms my entire holiday. God I love this stuff!

Postscript Postscript

This serendiptidy stuff really freaks me out. The book was finished and ready for a final proofreading, but I had to insert the following story.

Last week I went on holidays "out bush" with the family (Mudgee NSW to be specific). In Australia, "out bush" means anywhere away from the bigger cities and towns. We had an Airbnb property booked on a farm. We got there late in the day to find the property had been double booked. Also, unbeknownst to us, there was a food and wine festival that night. It was the busiest night of the year, and there was no alternative accommodation available for a hundred miles. Things were looking pretty grim. "Luckily" (yes, what is "luck"?) the embarrassed property owner managed to find two rooms in a small country town (Gulgong) thirty minutes' drive away. The people who had booked the rooms had car trouble, and had cancelled only minutes before.

The property was clean enough, but the beds were average. I woke up about 6 a.m. and decided to look around town while the family slept. In Sydney, population 4,526,479, you can get a good cup of coffee early in the morning pretty much anywhere. In Gulgong, population 2,521, your chances are a little less good. So (if you're a coffee lover) you can imagine my excitement to a) find any sort of food store open, and b) to find that they had an espresso coffee machine.

So I'm standing outside this café gazing up and down a deserted street wondering which way to walk. To my knowledge, the only two people awake were me and the guy who made my coffee (the store was empty of customers). At that moment, a door opened and a man walks towards a garbage bin. He seems surprised to see anyone on the street and smiles at me. (This is country Australia, not New York. People smile at each other out bush). I smile back and offer an appropriate comment: "G'day. Cracker of a morning."

For some reason we each sensed the other was up for a yarn, so we met in the middle of the street (Gulgong, population 2,521—we weren't in a lot of danger). I'll cut to the chase. I soon discovered the guy wrote and illustrated comic books, and had also self-published two books (one fiction, one non-fiction). I'd just received a cover for the book the day before, and was looking at my self-publishing options.

Seriously, how does this shit happen? How many self-published authors and illustrators do you think are walking the streets of Australian country towns at 6 a.m. in the morning? I'll help you out here: not many. And what are the chances of meeting such a person at the exact moment in a thirty-year writing project that it would be useful for me to talk to a self-published author and illustrator? We ended up talking for over an hour and he gave me some invaluable advice. He was also kind enough to sign his book for my daughter and give her inspiration and good advice for her first novel (a chip off the old block, my little Sophie).

The series of events that happened to put me across a street from this guy in the middle of nowhere at dawn astounds me. It all could have been for naught, however, if I hadn't been paying attention to the world around me, or if I hadn't followed my instincts and initiated a conversation. So pay attention to the world around you.

Trans-American Journey Analogy

You're driving along, you catch some place out of the corner of your eye, and feel a strong desire to pull over for lunch. There's no good reason to stop there, but you have a hunch. And it turns out to be a great hunch. Go figure.

→ in summary

Keep an open mind. Be receptive to the messages that life is giving you. Look at coincidences as possible opportunities for learning. Be aware always that life may be trying to tell you something, and listen.

3.11 Be an Inspiration

My grandmother inspired me. I lived with her for six months when I was thirteen, when my parents moved to the Outback, and then from age eighteen to twenty-three, when I returned to Sydney to attend university.

In her nineties, Granny and a "young friend" (who was in her late eighties) would take public transportation on a different outing every Saturday. They did that for twenty or thirty years. They'd catch buses, trains, and ferries to go somewhere for lunch. They would often be the oldest people wherever they went. People would marvel at how active they kept themselves. At ages ninety-four and ninety, they became a little too fragile for public transportation, so they'd visit each other every Saturday. It's a wonderful story of friendship. I think they knew each other for more than seventy years. So, you see, something as simple as having a friend for a long time and enjoying their company can be inspiring.

I read a story about the first double amputee to climb to the top of Mount Everest. I find the determination to do that amazing. It just goes to show what's possible if you put your mind to it. It is inspiring. If I was an amputee, I'd be thinking maybe there aren't as many boundaries out there as I thought.

I was watching a TV show about the first female governor of a province in Afghanistan, Habiba Sarabi. After years of war and Taliban oppression, women's rights have seriously suffered. For years, girls weren't allowed to be educated. Now there is a local leader who is a woman and who has overcome considerable personal and political opposition. I was inspired by her story, but I can't comprehend what it must mean to the local girls to know that anything is now possible.

One of my patients takes in kids with difficult family lives for short periods of time. He's got a wife and kids of his own, and a busy business, but they find the time to help kids with problems. They don't foster or adopt them; I think it's more like a short-term refuge. When I ask him for more information, he is light on details and seems a little embarrassed about it. "We give them a normal life for a while and help straighten them out," he says, without elaborating. A great guy, and very inspirational.

There's a guy who collects money for the Salvation Army near my office every Friday. He's a nice guy who stands with a box to collect money. I find the Salvos to be very inspirational as a group. Great people who do a great job. This guy seems to embody their cause. He stands there smiling at everyone and exudes a desire to help people. I feel good about myself when I see him. I feel even better when I give him some money (see next chapter). I make a point of buying him a cup of coffee every time I see him.

I suppose the point of being an inspiration is that you get to make people feel better about themselves. You get to help people believe anything's possible. It's a whole lot easier to have morning tea with Granny and her friend Eunice than it is to climb Everest without a couple of legs, but the effect on others is the same. You may already be an inspiration to others without trying. Being the best you can be is inspirational. Not accepting boundaries is inspirational. Being a good person is inspirational. Doing the most you can for others is inspirational. Being good at your job is inspirational. Helping people is inspirational. Living your dream is inspirational. Hell, just being happy is inspirational.

Try to inspire someone with what you do. Through some action, try to be the sort of person who makes others feel good. This sounds difficult, but it doesn't have to be. There are so many people out there with inspiring stories that I think we should all set our sights on being one of those people. Friends and colleagues of mine were kind enough to suggest that my positive attitude during radiotherapy for neck cancer was inspirational. Personally, I don't think I had any other option, but it's nice to know my adversity helped others.

Look around at the people who inspire you? What is it about them? I'm not talking about famous people; I'm talking about everyday normal people. The ones you look at and talk to and think, "Isn't that fabulous." What can you do to inspire others?

Trans-American Journey Analogy

You're driving along and you see some old guy on a Harley. He looks like he's about 110 and he's got a smile on his face you couldn't disrupt with a Taser. How does he make you feel?

in summary

Be the sort of person who inspires others.

3.12 Give Something Good Away

You can't REALLY give anything away. Try to give kindness away. It won't be gone for long. Try to be thoughtful, try to be loving, try to be caring with the intention of getting nothing in return. It's not going to happen. It's all going to come back like a well-flung boomerang.

You see, everything good comes back. You can't be nice to people without one of two things happening: Either they will be nice to you, or you will feel great about being nice to them. Win-win. Try being kind to people without getting anything in return. It may be your intention, but you'll get a positive return whether you want it or not.

A good friend of mine (let's call her Karen Savins of Crump Street in Mortdale to protect her identity) asked me for advice on how to help one of her students. The student had a difficult upbringing, through no fault of his own, and Karen had taken a personal interest in him. He'd always had a dark and broken front tooth. Karen took it upon herself to make sure it was fixed before he finished high school. She wanted to know which waiting list he could be put on in our government-funded system to have the work done.

Now, if a friend asks me for a favor, I don't hesitate. However, I admit I was very selfish with this request. I knew it would take me forever to figure out the appropriate channels to get the job done properly. I could do it myself in half the time and with a tenth of the frustration than it would take to navigate the bureaucracy. So, I said to Karen, "Don't worry, I'll do it myself."

This decision had some interesting consequences. Karen felt good about me because I was helping the kid she felt so strongly about. I felt good about Karen because she was going out of her way to help someone. How can you not admire and respect and be inspired by that? The kid's response was what got me thinking, though. He said to Karen, "Why would someone who doesn't know me want to help me?" I found that idea incredibly sad. Karen's response was something like, "He's my friend, and because I think you're worth it, that's good enough for him." That statement is a discussion in itself, but friendship is about believing in your friends (among a hundred other things).

Anyway, helping that one kid felt so much better than whatever it cost me to do it. The less you expect in return, the more you get. If you help a friend, there is the possibility that they will help you one day. In that sense, helping a friend could be considered an investment. But when it comes to helping a stranger, you have no such expectation, which is possibly why it feels so good. It's a wonderful paradox: The less you expect, the more you get.

But there is a dark side to giving things away. Just as you can't give away good things without getting good things back, you can't give away bad things without getting bad things back. Positive is repaid with interest and negative is repaid with interest.

You pat a dog, it licks you. You kick a dog, it bites you. Life is the same way. If you're the sort of person who spews negativity into the world (we all do at times) then it will be returned to you with interest. Why are positive people successful and negative people unsuccessful? Why do kind people seem so happy and unkind people seem so unhappy? Have you ever seen the Dalai Lama interviewed? Or Nelson Mandela? Or Mother Teresa? You could light a city with the glow of kindness and goodwill they project. Have you ever seen a murderer or a hardened criminal interviewed? Did you ever get a chilling feeling? It's almost like a black hole, sucking all goodness and kindness into a vortex of negativity.

So, you have to be very careful. Giving away goodness is easy. Donate to charities, donate your time, give away whatever you can. But we all suffer downs in life with the ups. You need to be very careful to not dwell too long in the downs; otherwise, negativity takes hold and becomes a self-fulfilling prophecy. If you feel down, force yourself to do something for someone. Get attached to an upward spiral of positive emotion.

Trans-American Journey Analogy

If you see someone by the side of the road you can help, do it.

---

in summary

Give away as much as you can (money, time, kindness, anything positive) and marvel at the interest you receive. Be careful to avoid, whenever possible, giving away anything negative.

3.13 Live in the Past Now (Reminiscing in the Present)

What are those magic moments in your past, your fond memories? Did you recognize when they occurred how special those moments were? Did you realize at the time that you would remember the moment for the rest of your life? There are lots of magic moments in your life. The trick is to recognize them when they happen and enjoy them in that moment. It might be a meal with a good friend, or time with a parent, or time with a child, or time with your wife. It could be anything. If you can realize it's a special moment at the time, you can REALLY enjoy it.

I went to see Bruce Springsteen a couple of years ago in Sydney. Sadly, Bruce doesn't come to Australia much and I'm a big fan. I knew it would be a moment I would remember forever, so I was in a frame of mind to enjoy it at the time. I knew it was going to be a great memory.

This is a hard concept to absorb while you're reading, because chances are reading this paragraph is not going to be one of those magic moments (I hope it is, but I doubt it). The trick is to keep your mind receptive to when those moments occur and wallow in the greatness of them. You won't know what I'm talking about until the next one comes along.

My life is filled with magic moments because I've got two little daughters. I watch people look at my children and I can tell they are fondly remembering their own children at that age. Well, I don't want to be one of those people who only remembers the good days. I want to enjoy the good days NOW (one of the virtues of being impatient). It's very easy. At least a couple of times a week something happens when I KNOW this is one of those great moments.

I've perfected this technique to the point where even the wind in the trees or the sunshine on my face can bring me great joy. All you have to do is pause for a few seconds and appreciate how wonderful life is.

Even an average existence can be filled with amazing memories. My father-in-law looks back fondly on his working life. I'll bet he didn't enjoy it that much when he was working. But he does now. Why not enjoy it more when you're there? All it takes is a little attitude shift. You just need to keep reminding yourself, "These are the good times," and start enjoying them more. It's a matter of perspective and relativity.

You're in the best years of your life. At least that's how it will seem in a couple of years. Well, if it's going to seem like that in a couple of years, why not start acting like that now?

Trans-American Journey Analogy

The scenery you're looking at, the diner you're eating in, may well be the best of the entire trip. Enjoy them like it never gets better than this.

→ in summary

Look for those moments each day that will seem like magic moments when you look back on your life. Enjoy them as much now as you will in the years to come. Reminisce now, not later. Realize that these are the best times of your life and suck as much enjoyment out of each day as you can.

3.14 Accept Responsibility and Move On

A theme pervading this book is that you're in control of your own destiny. "Ah, but Brett," you say, "What about that serendipity stuff? You said life was guiding me." Yes, I did say that, didn't I? Well, I think most people have unlimited potential. Even the people who seem to be disadvantaged have unlimited potential (look at Stephen Hawking, for instance). We set limits on ourselves, which is why in the second chapter I encouraged you to have a series of grand visions. Life may be guiding you, but it certainly isn't limiting you. Life will guide you to the top of Mount Everest (metaphorically speaking) whereas most people only let it guide them to the top of a compost mound. OK, I'm being melodramatic for effect, but we limit ourselves a whole lot more than life limits us. And why is that?

I think it's because we don't take full ownership or responsibility for our lives. We have this attitude that some third party or outside influence is somehow preventing us from getting ahead. The barriers are in our heads, not ahead of us. Damn, that was a good line. I'm going to repeat it: The barriers are in our heads, not ahead of us.

"So, what's the solution?" you ask. Take responsibility for whatever is wrong with your life and either fix it or move on. Until you accept that you are responsible for what happens to you (to a large extent) then you are doomed to being a victim. Either fix the problem if you can (and you generally can) or move on.

It is so tempting NOT to take responsibility, to blame something or someone else. It's easier to say the business is failing because the employees aren't motivated than to say the business is failing because you weren't taking responsibility. To say "My wife doesn't love me" is easier than admitting that maybe you take her for granted and aren't nice to her. Saying "My kids aren't well disciplined" is a way to avoid the possibility that you don't discipline them enough.

These examples are simplistic and a problem may in fact not be your responsibility, but you should attack every problem with the assumption that it IS your responsibility, and that you are the ONLY person who has a chance to fix it. It's a hard fact to accept.

Mrs. Taylor and I had a little "time out" period about seven or eight years into our marriage. We'd been fighting about her job and how hard she was working. Eventually, we separated. Anyway, it was one of the defining moments of my life. I loved her very much (still do), but I was unhappy. Something was going wrong with our marriage and it needed fixing. Of course, I assumed I was in the right. She was working long hours, not getting paid well, and had no potential for advancement. If only she would see reason, I thought, we could save our marriage.

There are two sides to every disagreement, and for some inexplicable reason both sides normally think they're right. Don't tell me you don't think you're right when you have an argument. But guess what? Someone is normally in the wrong.

You can't change someone else, you can only change yourself. Luckily (or was it luck?), I went to a course and had one of those serendipitous experiences in which the error of my ways was made clear to me. In an instant, I realized that I was the problem.

Accepting this fact was great because it meant that I was in control of the solution. I set about correcting my faults, or at least as many as I could. Eventually we got back together and have been living happily for more than eighteen years and two children later.

I'm living happily ever after because I believed I had control of my own destiny. I'm in control of my own destiny because I always look to myself as the source of most problems. It may seem harsh and negative, but it's a good thing. If I assume that all problems are of my own creation, then I have the ability to correct those problems. If I believe my problems are caused by someone else, what power do I have to fix them?

Read those last two sentences again because they're very important.

So, accept responsibility. Start with the assumption that all problems are your own fault, which means you have the ability to fix them. If you've made a mistake, accept that and move on. Nothing is ever gained by blaming others. You have a long journey ahead and it's important to keep moving.

Trans-American Journey Analogy

You're the driver, and you're the one steering. If you hit a pothole, whose fault is that? Even when someone else does something inexplicable, like falling asleep and crossing onto your side of the road, you still have the power and ability to be attentive and to avoid the accident.

in summary

Assume that every problem in your life is your fault and that you have the ability to fix it.

3.15 Put Yourself in the Other Person's Shoes

There's a little part of me that would love to be a hard-nosed businessman. You know the type: take no prisoners, win at all costs, all-conquering; that sort of thing. There is, however, a much larger part of me that wonders how the hell those people live with themselves.

My philosophy is that you should at all times consider what repercussions your actions and decisions will have on others. What is your gain, and what is the other person's loss? The other person doesn't have to be a person. It can be an animal, the environment, or anything. What are you getting, and what is the cost?

I had an employee, a young girl who was a single mother struggling to make ends meet. We had to restructure the business because the other dentist retired, and she was under-employed. What was I supposed to do? Fire a single mother and put her on the street? I couldn't do that. If I fired her, I would have made a little more money. But what would the consequences have been for her? She would have had no money for food, she would have lost her home, her son would have suffered, she might have lost her car, and she would have fallen behind on her credit card payments. Her life would have gone to crap. And why? So I could make a little more profit? Obviously, her net loss was greater than my net gain. Had I fired her, I wouldn't have been able to live with myself.

I used to be a sarcastic bastard. I had a sharp wit and a sharp tongue. In a group of people, I'd often find an opportunity to make a joke at someone else's expense. Many years ago, a friend of mine said, "I used to hate it when you made fun of me, but then I realized that you were doing it to everyone, so I just laughed with everyone else."

At the time, my sarcasm made me feel good. Now the concept horrifies me. What was my net gain from making fun of others? I'd get a laugh. I'd feel good about being the center of attention. What was the other party's net loss? They would feel belittled. Was my net gain more important than that person's net loss? Of course not. It was a horrible thing to do. I've still got a sharp tongue, but I pick on myself now. Self-deprecating humor is my stock-in-trade, and everyone gets to laugh at me, not someone else.

When I'm driving and in a hurry for some important reason (I almost never am, but let's pretend), then I might cut someone off or push my way into a line of cars, or I might not let someone merge in front of me. When I'm not in a hurry, I'm a shining example of auto politeness.

Why would I annoy someone on the road for no reason apart from being an extra couple of seconds closer to my destination? How can I justify upsetting other drivers, raising their blood pressure, and dispelling their faith in other humans through discourteous behavior just to save a little time? Complete madness. If people TRULY considered the consequences of their actions on others, would they always adopt the same actions?

So, here's your homework. Spend the next twenty-four hours analyzing everything you do, and I mean everything. Do any of your actions have a negative consequence on others? Is your net gain worth their net loss?

I think I project a "busy businessman" persona. Perhaps it's the coat and tie, because it's not the finely chiseled look of gravitas on my face. When I'm at the deli, older (presumably retired) people will offer to let me cut in line. I can only assume that they think I'm busy and have no time to waste, whereas they do have time on their hands. Normally I don't accept the offer because I'm never as busy as I look.

There was a time, however, when I used to accept the opportunity: when my daughters were with me. When they were little girls, the mischief twins (my daughters) could just about destroy the nicely stacked condiments section if they had to wait too long. Getting to the front of the line in those situations was a critical matter.

You can extend this concept to inanimate objects, such as the environment. What are the consequences of my actions on the environment? If I throw a piece of rubbish in the river, I don't have to worry about it. But what are the repercussions? Is the time I save in not handling rubbish properly offset by the impact on the environment? Of course not.

From 1946 to 1993 they would drop nuclear waste in the ocean. Out of sight, out of mind, apparently. The reasoning, I assume, was that it would cost too much to dispose of it otherwise. So, "too much" is weighed against whatever the hell the consequences are of nuclear waste in oceans?

We all make daily decisions that have negative impacts on people, animals, and nature. We all have to eat. Animals die so carnivores can live. Plants die so the vegetarians can live. When I drive to work, there is impact on the environment. All the toys and gadgets I love are produced with environmental consequences. It would be nice if our actions never had a detrimental effect on others, but that isn't going to happen. But if we all at least consider the effects, it should be possible to limit the damage. Every journey starts with the first step.

Trans-American Journey Analogy

Is it really going to kill you to let that guy merge into your lane? Do you really need to drive across the country in a tank? What if you had to store all those greenhouse gases in your own house? Consider the consequences of your actions. Look at the big picture. Stop thinking only about yourself.

in summary

Consider the effects of your actions on others. Try to put yourself in the shoes of the other person. Is your net gain worth their net loss?

Section 4

Challenges
(The Road Hazards)

W e've cleaned up our mental house, planned some exciting destinations, and gone over the rules for our grand journey. In this section, we're going to look at potential hazards, the things that may disrupt the trip: potholes, road construction, kangaroo and wombat crossings—that sort of thing.

I'm a dentist living in suburban Sydney. It takes me about ten minutes to drive to work. I've been doing the same trip for the last twenty years. When I back out of my garage, I have to be careful of people coming up quickly from behind. About fifty meters down the road there's what Australians call a "traffic calming" construction. It forces drivers to maneuver through a serpentine pattern in the road to slow them down. Why the hell those things are called "traffic calming" escapes me, because I feel anything but calm when I'm trying to negotiate them.

Another fifty meters along there's a speed bump that I have to take slowly or I bump the front of my car (it's low in the front). I can go over this particular speed bump a lot faster in my wife's car than in mine. The first corner I come to, there are often cars coming up from the left, so I need to be careful. Around the corner there's a school, so if I go to work later than normal, I have to watch out for the kids. There's a street on the right where idiots have twice pulled out in front of me and almost rammed me. It must be hard to see things in that direction in the morning, or stupid people live down that street. There are six roundabouts I negotiate at various speeds and two more speed bumps, one I can go over quickly, and one I have to go over slowly. There's only one set of traffic lights at that location, but it's very accident prone as people come down a hill on the left. They often accidentally run the red light. I always slow down and look left, even if the light is green. I almost got killed there once. (I was literally two seconds away from death.)

So, what's the point of this little ramble? To glorify the minutia of my mundane, middle-aged and balding middle-class existence? No. Because I drive the same way to work every day, I know what to look out for. I know where I can go a little faster and where I should go a little slower. I know where I need to be more careful, and I know the place I'm most likely to get killed if I'm inattentive. In short, I know what hazards to expect.

It's the same with your life. You're on the big journey, the grand trip. There are going to be hazards. There are things you need to look out for.

Every day on my trip to work I'm aware of the likely hazards and the less likely hazards. I don't expect a gorilla to leap from an overpass onto the roof of my car, but I do keep an eye out for the unexpected. The unexpected, however, doesn't occur as much as the expected, which makes my life easier because I can prepare better for the challenges of my daily drive to work.

As you read the hazards I've identified, I want you to ponder this question: Is this a problem I'm susceptible to? Some things will resonate at the moment, some will not. All of them are dangerous.

So let's get you a little more prepared for the likely challenges in the journey that is your life.

4.1 Being Negative

There are two people who live inside your subconscious mind. One is a sweet-faced, kind, empathetic cheerleader. The other is an evil, pernicious, old grouch with a hangover. These two people whisper in your ear all day every day. Which of the two you listen to will determine how your life turns out. How scary is that?

I love listening to the cheerleader. I love what she's got to say. When I'm feeling good she's telling me I can do anything. That is the voice I try to listen to. That is the voice I try to encourage. The problem is, I don't always feel good. Some days are harder than others. Some years are harder than others. Some lives are harder than others. And when things aren't going well, that's when the evil grouch generally starts giving you advice.

Do you ever catch yourself thinking thoughts like these?

"I don't feel well."

"I'm tired."

"I'm sick of this job and I need a vacation."

"I'm broke."

"I don't know how I'm ever going to do it. I'm just not good enough."

"I just know something's going to go wrong."

"I know they're going to be disappointed."

"I wish I hadn't done that. These things always happen to me."

"If only…"

Yes, if only. If only you could make the evil grouch shut up. Every negative thought you have is your subconscious mind trying to rain on your parade. The cheerleader is taking a nap and the evil grouch is piping in with some unwelcome advice. Your challenge is not to take that advice. Your challenge is to listen to the positive thoughts and ignore the negative ones. Your challenge is to put a mental gag around the mouth of the evil grouch.

Your life is not going to be fabulous twenty-four hours a day. It's not supposed to be. If it were, it would be very boring. You need a few downs to make the ups more enjoyable (we covered that before). You need, however, to pick yourself up as quickly as possible from the downs or you run the risk of staying down. When things aren't going according to plan, be AWARE of the negative thoughts. They are a hazard in your life. If you are aware of them you can deal with them safely and in time (with practice) reprogram your subconscious mind. It is a hazard that is easier to avoid if you are aware it exists. Don't take negative thoughts for granted.

I've got a few ongoing health problems. I get a few symptoms that annoy me and bring me down a little. The pain is an opportunity for the negative thoughts to creep in. I think to myself, "That's sore; I wish I didn't get these problems." I used to let the evil grouch continue to comment on my life. "How come I get these problems? It's not fair. Why can't I be like healthy people?" And before I realize it, there's a whole negative speech going on in my head about what a crappy life I have.

A strategy I've recently adopted is to give the negative voice Billy Connolly's Scottish accent. I also let him comment on my negativity in a Billy Connolly sort of way. So, say I get the thought that I'm sick of working so hard. I then replay that thought with Billy speaking: "Oh for fook sake, you cry baby. Can you just try to suck it up for me a wee bit." Doing this acts as a circuit breaker. The negative thoughts immediately pass. But better still, now I've got a smile on my face. Try it yourself. Pick a voice you can't take seriously and apply it to the negative voice in your head.

Your life is what you believe it is. If you listen to the negative speech in your head, then that is what you become. If you listen to the positive, then that is what you become. It is your subconscious mind that offers negative advice. You can use your conscious mind to overrule that advice and in time reprogram your subconscious to only offer positive advice. You have the power to decide whom to listen to.

When you get a negative thought, recognize it for what it is—an unwanted comment—and move on. Don't let it become a constant conversation that brings you down. Look out for the hazard and guard against it.

Possibly a more dangerous voice than the one in your head is the one in your mouth. Being negative to yourself is bad enough, but being negative to others is a serious crime.

Constructive criticism is like a constructive beating. It still hurts.

Have you ever felt perfectly well and then someone comes up to you and says, "Are you feeling OK? You don't look so good." What happens then? Suddenly you don't feel as well as you thought you did. This demonstrates the immense power of suggestion. Plant a seed of negativity and it starts to grow. People suddenly start second-guessing themselves for no good reason. I heard a great quote once that went something like this: "Don't walk through my clean mind with your dirty feet." That's what negativity is.

Think of your mind like a sailing ship, slowly being blown in the correct direction by a gentle breeze. We have lots of challenges in life (fewer, I hope, after you read the book) and sometimes the breeze disappears. Then we're left wallowing in the ocean. Negativity is a big gust of wind trying to push you off course. If your goals are good enough, you won't be blown off course because you will be sure of your direction. But not everyone is that lucky. Some people only have a fragile hold on their lives. Do you really want to be the one who breaks someone's spirit, the person who breaks a person's resolve and blows them off course?

Negativity has no good purpose ever, be it directed inward or outward. Don't allow your own negative thoughts to sprout and grow. And don't direct negative thoughts at others. Find a positive spin every time you are tempted to be negative. If you think someone doesn't look well, then tell them they look great. That may be enough to pick up his or her spirits. Praise and encouragement starves negativity. Praise and encouragement deprives the evil grouch of his strength. Encourage the cheerleader in your head and give strength to the cheerleaders in everybody else's head. I know you can do it.

Trans-American Journey Analogy

Negative thoughts are the potholes in your life. You can hit a few without doing too much damage, but it's best to avoid them.

> → in summary
>
> Silence the negative voices in your head and don't be a negative voice in someone else's head.

4.2 Being Critical

If you manage to expunge negativity from your existence as you would cast a soiled diaper in the garbage (can you tell I wrote this bit when the kids were little?), then being critical won't be an issue. It's worth discussing though.

Being critical is an active form of negativity. Being negative might mean you say to someone, "You don't look so well." Being critical is attempting to justify your position of negativity. "You don't look well. Your eyes are bloodshot and your skin is pale. It looks like you're not eating well and you don't get enough exercise and you work too hard and . . ." Well, you get the idea.

Being critical happens when you've taken a personal interest in reinforcing the negativity. A negative comment might be something like, "That won't work." A critical comment will be an explanation about why it won't work. It's negativity with feeling. It's negativity with purpose and reason.

None of it is necessary. Focus on the positive. If your friends don't eat well, show them how to cook a good meal. If they don't exercise, invite them to come and do something active with you. If you really are 100 percent sure something isn't going to work, say, "That sounds great. I think it would be even better if we did this." Then steer them in a direction you think will work.

Be careful though. Some of the greatest advances have occurred when people didn't realize something was impossible and then proved it wasn't. I'm careful to never suggest something isn't possible. Unless it's going to cause serious injury, I'd prefer to be wrong than to discourage someone from attempting the impossible.

My pet-peeve in life is people who are critical of children. It really burns me up when I hear adults criticizing children. There is almost always a way to put a positive spin on any situation that seems adverse. My eldest daughter once found a pencil and drew a picture on the wall. Now, I can't say my wife and I were happy, but in her defense, it was a good picture. After telling her how lovely the picture was (because she was proud of it), we suggested it would be better to draw the pictures on paper. Did I really want to stifle her creativity at age four by being critical of her actions?

Look for the positive in every situation. Praise people even when they do something wrong, and then redirect their energies in a more positive direction. Everyone responds to encouragement better than discouragement. I know that isn't going to work every time, but if you start with the premise that it's possible, you'll find success more often than not. Give it a go.

Trans-American Journey Analogy

Being critical is like intentionally bumping into someone's car for no good reason. Keep your road rage to yourself. Better still, go over and polish the person's windshield so they can see the road ahead a little better.

→ # in summary

Being critical is actively being negative to someone. Instead of criticizing them, look for ways to encourage and redirect someone's energies in a positive direction.

4.3 Making Compromises

There's a juicy story about one of my more monumental screw-ups in this section, so you may want to keep reading.

There are two meanings for the word compromise. English must be the hardest language in the world to learn because it can be so ambiguous. Compromise can mean "settling a dispute by making concessions" or it can mean "expedient acceptance of standards that are lower than is desirable." I'm talking here about the second definition.

I don't know about the rest of you, but I generally know what the "right" thing to do is. If you know what the "right" thing to do is, and then you do something different, that's a compromise, and it's asking for trouble. Compromise makes life harder. It's easier to do things the right way.

Let's take a simple example like fixing something. There will always be the right way to do it, and every other way. There may be a couple of right ways that work equally well. Then there are the compromises, the shortcuts that will lead to a less satisfactory outcome, or lead to short-term success but with long-term failure.

Every shortcut, every compromise, requires a careful evaluation to have a chance of success. You have to weigh the risk against the benefit, the likelihood of failure, the time and money saved with a compromise versus the cost of redoing something if it doesn't work, the reduced lifespan of the compromise, that sort of thing. It's all mental effort you don't need. That's stress you don't need. If you don't compromise, if you do the right thing, there is no stress. The right thing is the right thing. Sure, it will take longer, but there is no emotional cost to pay.

If the decision to be made is a moral one, then the consequences of compromise are even greater. When you compromise your integrity, when you compromise your ethics, then you really start to complicate your life. And we at Brett Taylor Publishing are not about compromising and complicating, are we? No, we're about simplifying.

The right thing is always going to be the right thing, at least from your perspective. Not everyone will have the same ethics or moral constraints, but we're not talking about everyone; we're talking about you. And YOU always know what the right thing to do is, at least by your own standards. Being true to yourself is a great way to simplify your life.

I'm not a saint by any stretch of the imagination. My journey in writing this book has required me to take a good, hard, long look at myself on numerous occasions, and I haven't always liked what I saw (even ignoring the increasing size of my forehead). My imperfections have allowed me to refine my philosophies (that's my spin on it anyway). I try to follow my own rules, but I've made all the mistakes that have produced the rules. I'll give you an example of a compromise that plays on my mind.

We bought a house a few years back. During the negotiations, we agreed on a price with the sellers. While I was getting the financing organized, another buyer became interested and the seller reneged on the deal with us. I really wanted the house, so I offered more money. We got the house, but it ended up costing me a lot more. The seller compromised his integrity to get more money. That was his issue not mine, but it put me in a difficult financial situation. I had to stretch myself more than I wanted.

Then I had to sell the house I had been living in. The market was dropping and it looked like I would be in a worse situation, getting less than I had expected for my house. I ended up (luckily) with two people interested. I agreed to a price with one person, and then used that fact to leverage a higher price out of the second party. It worked perfectly (from a financial perspective), but I compromised my integrity. The first person thought they'd bought their dream home and I pulled the rug out from under them. The second party was forced to pay more than they wanted (like me) for their dream home. I doubt either of them were happy, and it was my fault. I needed the money and I manipulated the situation to achieve my goal. I didn't do anything legally wrong, but I feel I did the wrong thing by my own standards. I had all sorts of justifications at the time, but the fact that I'm writing about it proves I know it was the wrong thing to do and that it still plays on my mind. The value of the house I sold, however, has gone up considerably more than the house I bought. Maybe that's a karma thing. Who knows?

Compromises cause an emotional drain you don't need. If you built your own house and compromised on the construction, you would always be waiting for it to fall down. Do you really want that stress?

The same principle applies to lying. If you don't always tell the truth, you need to remember what lies you've told so that you can repeat them when necessary. How hard must that be? To be constantly in fear of saying the wrong thing because you're not sure which story you're supposed to repeat? That's not a simple life. Generally, you can get away with the truth no matter what the situation. Even if you have to spin the truth a little by putting a positive outlook on whatever you have to say, it's a lot easier than lying.

There are many situations in my working life in which I'm confronted with the need to give someone bad news. It might be that something has gone wrong because I've screwed up, or because it was harder than anticipated, or maybe it was just bad luck. I can always blame someone or something for most adverse outcomes, but then I have to make up a story and repeat that story later. It's too hard. When in doubt, tell the truth. When you're not in doubt, tell the truth anyway.

The world is not always black and white, right or wrong. I'd love to simplify things that much, but it's not going to happen. There are many times when there is no obvious "right" thing to do. Most wars fall into this category. Luckily most of us are not forced to make such difficult decisions as when to go to war. And even if we were, we'd still be required to do "the right" thing based on what we thought was the right thing.

You (yes, I'm talking to you personally) always know what the right thing to do is. I'm absolutely convinced of that. That's the other voice in your head—the professor. You've got the grouch telling you bad things, the cheerleader telling you good things, and the professor who knows the truth. The professor is your conscience. *SHe is always right for you. SHe knows the truth for you. The professor is the calm, reasoned voice in your head that knows you better than you know yourself. Sometimes the other two are so loud that you don't hear the professor. Sometimes the professor talks too softly, and sometimes you ignore the advice, but the voice is always there and it's always right for you (if you choose to listen).

Trans-American Journey Analogy

Do you want good quality parts in your car, or dodgy ones? Do you want good quality tires or cheap retreads? Are you prepared for the consequences of your cheap tires blowing out when you're driving fast down a crowded freeway? Are you taking shortcuts that may lead to disaster, or are you following a route that you know will get you to your destination?

→ in summary

When you compromise on anything, you are increasing the risk of failure in your life and increasing your stress levels. You don't need either of those things. There is a voice in your head (the professor) who always knows the right thing to do. Listen to that voice.

(* SHe is my way of being gender non-specific. Clever, eh?)

4.4 Making Excuses

Making excuses is the opposite of taking responsibility. If you take responsibility you won't be in the habit of making excuses.

It could just be that my perspective has changed as I've gotten older, but it seems that people take less responsibility for their actions these days. In our overly litigious (Western) society it always seems like someone else is responsible for anything that goes wrong.

There was a court case recently in which this guy was driving home drunk. He had two or three times the legal blood-alcohol limit. He crashed his car and got permanent injuries. Where he crashed, there were municipal road works underway, so he sued the municipality for not signposting the work well enough. It seems they didn't take into account the fact that drunk drivers at night might not be able to read signs properly (I'm serious). Anyway, he won and got millions of dollars. He was considered partly to blame (contributory negligence), so he only got part of the money, but he still got it. As a result, there will be added cost to the community so people behaving illegally don't hurt themselves. Absolute madness.

Society these days is sending out the message that there is always someone to blame, so it is easy to see why this mentality of making excuses has crept into conventional thinking. Making excuses and casting blame is an insidious evil, however, and something you need to protect against or you will never take charge of your life.

Things go wrong in life. Things don't go according to plan. The quickest solution is to pick yourself up, dust yourself off, and move on. Take responsibility, don't make excuses, and don't look for people to blame.

You know you are making excuses if you use the word "because" too often, as in "the work was late because . . .," or "I haven't done it because . . .," or "I missed the appointment because . . ."

You and I know there is always a REASON why things don't get done or adverse events happen, but is the reason a valid excuse? And is it good for your life to always find an excuse?

You see, an excuse is a cop-out. It is a way of looking for an external cause, when you should be looking within. It is a way of avoiding the real issue. It is a way of hiding when you shouldn't be hiding.

If you are in the habit of making excuses, then something is wrong. If your work is always late, then maybe you need to admit to yourself that you could be better organized. If that's the truth, then great; you have the opportunity to fix that problem. But if you try to hide behind a false reason (an excuse), then you never move on, you never take responsibility, and you never grow as a person.

Now, you may not even realize you're a serial excuse-maker. The habit may be so ingrained in your personality that you don't notice it. So, let's start by being conscious of the excuses you make, and the excuses others make to you. Have you made any excuses today? Have any been made to you?

If you find yourself in the middle of making an excuse, pause and try to find the real reason behind the excuse. The real reason is something that can be corrected. The excuse is uncorrectable because it places the blame beyond your control, which of course is the purpose of an excuse. If you're serious about moving forward with your life, you can't be a person who WANTS to make excuses. You'll want to be a person who desires to be in control of the solutions, because if you take control you can solve the problem. You can't rely on someone else to solve your problems. The person most interested in you is you, so take charge, and make no excuses, right?

Once you become attuned to excuses, they will start to sound lame. You will have trouble making them (because you will be ashamed to do it) and you will challenge others for making them (in a nice way, of course).

Trans-American Journey Analogy

I can't figure out how excuses fit into the analogy. They're a hazard, so let's work with that idea. Are they a pothole? No. A speed bump? No. A road block? Sort of. No. I've got it now. I was stalling, waiting for inspiration (that's an excuse; see how I artfully weaved that into the conversation?). Excuses are a detour. They divert you from your true destination. If you are making excuses, then something is wrong and it needs to be fixed. While you continue to make excuses, the real problem isn't getting fixed so you are diverted from your destination (a simplified life).

→in summary

Don't make excuses and don't accept excuses. Confront and fix the real reason behind the excuse.

4.5 Self Importance

I know more than one pompous arsehole. Most of them would never lower themselves to the point where they would read something I wrote, so I'm in no danger of offending them.

Self-importance is that state-of-mind in which you take yourself too seriously. The more you think you've progressed in status, the more you are at risk of self-importance. Notice I said, "the more you think you've progressed"; it's all about your own perception, not reality. You don't have to be a high-powered CEO or politician to exhibit symptoms; all it takes is a quorum of one person who hangs off your every word, and the scene is set.

The danger of self-importance is that you lose perspective. If you have a few successes in life, or get a little respect for whatever it is you do, it's easy to start magnifying or exaggerating your place in the world.

Egos can be very fragile, and most people crave encouragement and endorsement. While I'm all for encouraging people, I don't like encouraging people to think they are intrinsically better than anyone else.

The delicious irony of self-importance is that the people who really are the most important tend to be the humblest. The more important you REALLY are, the more likely you are to treat everyone as an equal.

The smartest person I've ever known reasonably well is Norm Thomas. Norm is an emeritus professor from the University of Alberta. He has a few doctorates, and is effectively a specialist in several professions. I'm convinced that Norm believes everyone is as smart as him. Norm is a gifted teacher who makes all his students feel like they can learn what he has learned, and understand what he understands. You could not meet a nicer, more encouraging, enthusiastic, and yet humble individual. Norm is in his early eighties. I assume he is at his intellectual peak, because I can't comprehend anyone being any smarter. He's a person who has the right to feel "self-important" from an intellectual standpoint, but he is as far from that state-of-mind as possible. I've met many imposing people over the years that exuded self-importance with good reason, yet none of them have impressed me like Norm, who exhibits no sense of self-importance.

The danger of self-importance is that you don't see yourself as you really are. How's that line go? "It's hard to be humble when you're perfect in every way." It's a funny line with a lot of truth in it. Losing perspective of your place in the world means you lose contact with who you really are. Deep down I don't think anyone is any better than anyone else. If I'm smarter than you, how is that any fault of mine? It's like suggesting I'm better than someone else because I'm taller. It makes no sense. People can't change how tall they are, and they can't change how smart they are. You can't believe you are better than anyone else because of something you had no control over (the abilities and attributes you were born with).

Sure, I'm impressed by an athlete who achieves great things with natural ability and single-minded determination. But can the athlete claim any credit for natural ability? I don't think so. Can the athlete claim any credit for single-minded determination? If that trait is in your makeup, how can you claim credit for it?

It's an interesting conundrum; we can all be "better," but if we DO apply ourselves to be "better," are we any better than the people who don't apply themselves? Is the ability to apply yourself a given, as your height is a given? It's all very interesting.

Which brings me back to the issue of perspective. I think you should be as good as you can be, but I don't think you should feel you are better than anyone else. If you're starting to feel self-important, you're probably starting to think you're better than other people, and you're not. You can claim no more credit for your station in life than you can for your height or your sex. Many random events have made you what you are, so how can you claim credit for any of them? You are what you are, which is great, but don't think it's because you're any better than anyone else.

There's an old saying: "You're never a prophet in your own village," which to me means, "It doesn't matter how clever the rest of the world thinks you are; your friends and relatives know what you're really like." If you're prone to feelings of self-importance, make sure you spend a bit of time with people who don't treat you like you're important. Tell your mother you're too important to help her with the washing up. Her response should give you a better perspective on who you really are.

Trans-American Journey Analogy

I was reading an article about the cars that the world's ten richest people drive. It wasn't an impressive list of cars (if you're a car enthusiast). Bill Gates has a Porsche, but its seven-years old. Most of the other wealthy people had nondescript, average cars. You see, if you are extremely rich, you don't need status symbols. If you really are important, then you don't need to act important.

→ # in summary

If you really are that important, there is no need to act important. If you aren't that important, you shouldn't be acting important. Let go of the need to feel important. We're all the same, we're all different, and we're all the same.

4.6. Overcommitting Time, Money, and Emotion

This topic is hard for me to write about because it has been, and probably continues to be, my greatest challenge. But, like I said before, I can only write this book because I've made all the mistakes I'm trying to help you correct or avoid. It's a self-help book for me first, and the rest of you people second. Anyway, if you want to know about the dangers of alcohol you don't ask a lifetime teetotaler; you ask a reformed alcoholic. I haven't made all the mistakes to test my theories, but I've developed all the theories because I've made all the mistakes.

My struggle is overcommitting. Man, that's a big mistake, and so easy to do. If you feel overwhelmed, you are probably overcommitted. If you're not feeling overwhelmed, be aware of the potential problem and guard against it.

My problem is that everything seems like a good idea. I love life and want as much of it as possible. The problem is (and I'm sure you people are smarter than me and already realize this) that the more you do, the less time you have to enjoy ALL the bits of your life.

This is how bad it got. I started with a full-time job as a dentist. I bought the business, so now I'm a business owner as well. I wanted to get better at my job, so I committed to significant study. I'd spend at least two hours studying at the end every workday. I'd also travel around the world to learn things. Then I decided to donate my spare time to my profession by serving on the council of our state dental association. I'd spend at least ten full days a year attending meetings plus many hours reading minutes, doing research, and developing ideas. Since 1991, I've assumed responsibility for organizing my local dental association meetings. Then I got asked to help with education, so I joined the board of an education body for dentists around Australia. Then a dental education body in the United States, where I studied advanced dental stuff, asked me to teach for them in Australia. So, I'd spend three weeks full-time every year doing that, and countless hours outside the three weeks preparing the students' cases and discussing treatment with them. I've got all these major projects in my practice to complete, such as the website, educational stuff for my own patients, business reorganization. Little things like that. Did I mention I'm a perfectionist? It all has to be done properly. Then a couple of kids came along who (rightly) demanded some of my time. Oh, and did I mention I'm trying to write a book?

Then I buy a big house because it was a great deal and my family was getting bigger and there's lots of things that need doing and now I've got two little people I want to spend more time with and no freakin' time to spend. Did I mention I'm trying to write a book, too? Is it any surprise it's taken me so long to write? No, it doesn't surprise me either.

So, what do you think? Am I an expert on overcommitting? Are you curious to find out what I did when I figured out that overcommitting was a bad idea?

Well, the first thing I did was to acknowledge that I have a problem (take responsibility). I wasn't going to make any excuses because I learned my own lessons well. I started dropping commitments without adding any. Previously I'd been like a juggler, adding more and more balls until I was franticly trying to keep them all aloft. Now that I recognize the problem, I don't add any more balls. Actually, that's an interesting analogy. Handling stress is like being a juggler. Some people can juggle nine balls, some seven, some five, some three, and some struggle to hold one ball without dropping it. If you're not juggling your life confidently and competently then you're probably overcommitted.

If you are overcommitted, try to prioritize what is important and what isn't. Just to give you a hint, anything to do with your family is important. Drop things that waste time and are not crucial to your journey. I liked donating time to my profession, but once I had kids I decided it was more important to donate my time to them.

Life changes, so don't waste your time on things you don't enjoy. I used to love playing golf. When I had kids, I wanted to spend more time with them. I aimed to spend less time playing golf, but I continued to play regularly with a few guys because I didn't want to let them down. Eventually, I moved on. Now I only play golf every now and then, not most weeks like I did before. Adding children to my life was important, so something had to go in order to make room for them.

Try not to overcommit financially. It is a mistake I have made and it has caused me years of unnecessary stress. If buying something is going to negatively impact your life, then have a big, long, hard think about whether it's a good idea or not. If buying that new car means you have to work longer and spend more time away from your family, then decide whether it's worth it. When I bought my new house, I made the excuse that the kids would love it. The truth, of course, is that they would prefer to see more of me in a cheaper house, than less of me (because I have to work harder) in the more expensive house.

Then there's the problem of emotional overcommitment. This is what you get when you can't let go of something. I didn't want to let go of being on the board of directors of my dental association because it made me a "big shot." Well it didn't, but I thought it did. Sometimes it's hard to move on because of weird attachments.

For years, I had the daily newspaper delivered. I'd make sure I read all of it every day, and I would keep sections for days so that I didn't miss anything. I've got friends with piles of newspaper sections they intend to read one day. Yeah, sure! If you're one of those people, do the recycling world a favor and donate your pile. I even used to get obsessive with TV shows. If I committed to a show, I wanted to watch every episode. If it started to get less interesting, I would still watch because I was committed. I enjoyed the first series of "Desperate Housewives" for a while, but then it became a chore to watch. I didn't let go of it as quick as I should have because of that strange emotional commitment.

FOMO (Fear of Missing Out) is a recently coined acronym that describes part of the problem. You people addicted to Facebook, Twitter, Instagram, or whatever other stupid social media phenomenon develops between now (my now) and when you read this will have a terminal case of FOMO. You will be suffering because you need to know what's going on all of the time. It's exactly like me having to read the entire newspaper every day. Different decades, same stupid problem.

I see social media as an ongoing and evolving, pernicious process to deny you full enjoyment of your life. I know that sounds harsh, but I predict the long-term effects of social media will bring considerable pain and suffering.

I was a kid in the 60s and 70s. In those days, television was the chief distraction from reality. In retrospect, I was probably guilty of watching too much TV. This is proven by my ability to remember the theme songs for *The Brady Bunch*, *The Adams Family*, and *Green Acres*. In defense of that era, at least when you unpinned yourself from television, you usually interacted with the real world. You'd go outside and play, or hang out with your friends (physically, not online).

The first major backward step after television (which was a backwards step itself in terms of interaction with the world) was the camcorder.

People no longer went on holidays and looked at the broad majesty of creation with awe and wonder. They went on holidays and looked at the broad majesty of creation through a three-inch viewfinder.

After the camcorder, the next backward step was the Sony Walkman. With that technology, you could walk down the street completely divorced from the sounds and experiences around you. Sure, you got to listen to the music you liked, but you weren't experiencing the real world in real time. Then we got the iPod, which gave us longer battery time and lots more songs. It was brilliant technology, but what are you giving up by spending your life just listening to music?

Now, in the social media era, it's worse. People only look at the view so they can figure out how to frame a selfie. How many photos have you seen in which you're looking at the view and the person who is actually at the view is staring at a six-inch square screen. So, that's meant to be progress? When you're on vacation, the size of the screen you're looking into has gotten bigger?

Social media is an addiction. You need to know that. It will steal your life in a heartbeat if you're not careful. The REAL world is everything you can see, hear, touch, and smell. It's not a screen. That's not real.

In pre-computer days, there were TV addicts who spent countless hours divorced from reality. This was widely considered to be unhealthy. In the computer era, the percentage of the population succumbing to screen addiction seems to be getting higher.

Studies suggest that social media is making people depressed. You get bombarded by your "friends" posting the highlights of their lives, and soon your life starts to seem inadequate. It presents a distorted view of reality, and gives us a distorted sense of community.

And then there's all of this "liking" rubbish. Too many people invest too much of their own self-worth in whether others are "liking" their comments. The world is becoming too needy. You don't need to be validated by others. If you've ever checked to see how many people "like" what you've said, you have become a victim. You are allowing others to control your happiness. It's not good, so don't let it happen.

The solution? Try to disconnect a little more. Try to engage with the physical world more, and with the cyber-world less. I could berate you for several more pages, but the solution is that simple. The world is outside. Disconnect from your screen and enjoy it a little more.

So, if you're a person who keeps taking on more and more until you are overwhelmed, then it's about time you cut back. Make a little room in your life for what's important, and eliminate the baggage you keep carrying out of habit. Reduce the time you spend trying to keep track of what the hell everyone you've ever met is doing every single moment of every single day. If you're having a great experience, immerse yourself in it and enjoy it for what it is. Don't squander it by trying to figure out how you can tell the world what you're doing. Live in the moment. If you commit to something new make sure it's worth the effort and the cost. Drop something else to make room if necessary. And remember, most things to do with your family are more important than most other things. Overcommitment is like background noise in your life. It is behind the scenes, nagging at you constantly. Until you free yourself of those burdens, you may find it difficult to relax.

Trans-American Journey Analogy

Overcommitting is like driving into a curve too fast. You have to hang on tight to avoid running off the road. If you do it too often, you WILL run off the road.

> ➤ # in summary
>
> Don't overcommit your time, money, or emotion. If you are over-committed and overwhelmed, start dropping things without adding anything. Figure out what's important and what you enjoy, and let go of the rest. Don't just keep doing things out of habit if they are no longer satisfying.

4.7 Isolation (Lack of Community)

It may not be a concept you're comfortable with, but you and I are animals. Sure, we look a little different than Rover over there in the corner, and I'd like to think that most of us smell better; but, like it or not, we're all animals. If you can accept that (and I can), then you have to accept that all animals have certain needs. The obvious ones are air, water, and food. A less obvious one is community.

We humans are pack animals. We like to live in groups. Being in a group has advantages, evidenced by the fact that our cities are getting bigger and bigger, and there are more of them. Like the rest of you, I enjoy time away from people every now and then, but it takes a very special person to be able to cut themselves off from human contact for any length of time, and you and I aren't that special. If you were that special, you wouldn't be reading this book; you'd be in a cave somewhere. Because community is a necessity, we can't (and shouldn't) escape it. Isolation is a bad thing and should be guarded against and avoided.

I suggest there are three communities to which you belong: family, work, and interests, and there are various subsets of these three groups. For example, I have the following communities and subsets:

1. Family

    a) Immediate family (wife and kids)

    b) Wife's side of family

    c) My side of family

2. Work

    a) My workplace, patients and team members, suppliers, etc.

    b) Colleagues who don't work with me but who I see at meetings

    c) Colleagues I interact with in email groups

3. Interests

    a) Old friends (school and people since school)

    b) New friends (mostly met because they have kids our age)

    c) Cycling buddies

To me, a community is a peer or family group with shared interests or history.

So, what's the danger of isolation and why should it be avoided? Well, it's the danger of disconnection, of being out of touch with your peers, of being out of touch with your roots. In a community, shared problems are reduced and shared successes are magnified. You hear less from the bad voices in your head when you are in a community because you can share your fears and exorcise them, or at least put them in a better perspective.

Let me give you an example of the benefits of community and the dangers of isolation. Dentistry isn't the easiest job in the world. There are many challenges and frustrations. If I'm having trouble mastering a technique, or having problems with specific equipment or materials, I can share those problems with my dental community (usually I do this with an e-mail group of my peers). It might be that everyone has the same problem for which there is no solution. If I was isolated, I'd continue to think I was an idiot for having that problem. I might start listening to the negative voices in my head. Just knowing I'm not alone eases the burden of "failure" because it's not just me that has the problem. It is no special fault of mine. Or perhaps the problem I was experiencing was shared by many, but solved by others. My community provides me with the tools to overcome my frustration. They either tell me I'm not alone, or they help me solve my problem. So, community is about more than proximity to people; it's about proximity to the support of people, proximity to commonality of purpose, thinking, and emotion.

The internet allows us to solve problems these days in a way that was unimaginable just a generation ago. No, I haven't suddenly fallen in love with Facebook. Scrolling through some user forum to find out why your phone reception is poor in a certain locality is not the same as being bored rigid by photos of what people you barely remember had for lunch today.

I will, however, grudgingly admit that for some people social media may solve their feelings of isolation. If it's working for you, and you have no reservations, then sure, find your place in an online community. Be very careful though. I think social media has a strong potential to create and encourage isolation. I will always maintain that being with someone physically is a lot different than being with someone virtually. There is no emoticon that can replace a gentle touch on the shoulder from a friend when you've just lost a loved one.

You can easily become isolated through poor decisions or bad luck. A petty fight with a family member that never gets settled can lead to isolation. I have a friend who has not spoken to her sister in years. They had a fight over almost nothing and neither apologized, so now they don't talk. When you're in the middle of these fights they seem important; however, to an independent observer they seem stupid. Both are now isolated through what I consider to be foolish pride.

If you read chapter 1 (if you didn't what are you doing here?), then you will appreciate that I am concerned about family isolation. Family bonds are critical to a healthy mental attitude. Don't allow yourself to become isolated from your family, or if you do, make sure you are conscious of, and comfortable with, the ramifications. When the person from whom you are isolated dies, will you be happy or sad? Are you happy to imagine that person dying without your differences being sorted out? If you're comfortable with the dispute never being resolved, and if you think you will happily live the rest of your life knowing there was no hope of salvaging that relationship, then great. If you think there will be the tiniest bit of guilt gnawing at you for not trying harder to patch up the differences, then maybe it's time to bury the hatchet. If you try and fail, at least you will always be able to console yourself for having tried. If not, well, I don't think it's healthy to live with those burdens. If it's too late (the person has died), then you need to let go, like I explained in chapter 1. It is, however, easier to never have the problem than it is to solve it.

It's the same with all your communities, not just family. If you become isolated, life gets harder. Fortunately, during our married life my wife and I have usually had fabulous, supportive neighbors. At our last house, however, one of our fabulous neighbors moved and we ended up with less-than-fabulous neighbors. We tried our best, but the relationship broke down. It was a burden to even sit in our backyard in case we had to confront them. It was not a lot of fun and we eventually moved (we were thinking about moving anyway). If we had intended on staying in that house, we would have had to settle that difference one way or another. You can't move from your family, but you can move from your neighbors. If you keep having neighbor disputes, you should look within not without.

Trans-American Journey Analogy

There something comforting about sharing your journey with people who have similar interests. If you're riding a Harley on your trip with a bunch of other people riding Harleys, and if something goes wrong, you will have well-qualified people around you to help.

→ in summary

Shared interests and shared history with others helps to dilute problems and multiply successes. Maintain good connections with all the communities in your life. Repair damage as soon as possible.

4.8 Expectation

Have you ever almost killed someone? I almost killed a family of three (and myself) because I wasn't aware of the dangers of "expectation."

It happened like this. A friend of mine from the United States was in Australia lecturing. He came with his wife and stepson. They had a few days free and I was driving them around the Australian countryside to see the sights. We'd had a great time, but the candle was being burned at both ends and we were all sleep deprived. On the final day, we watched the Phillip Island fairy penguins at dusk and then had dinner.

It was about 10 p.m., I was exhausted, and we still had a three-hour drive back to our hotel. About an hour into the return trip, as the other three slept, I began to struggle to stay awake. If I had been alone, I would have pulled over to the side of the road for a nap. This was obviously a disaster waiting to happen, but because I didn't want to disappoint anyone by delaying the trip home, I pressed on.

The inevitable happened and I nodded off. Luckily, I drifted onto the gravel shoulder and woke up. The car went into a slide. When I corrected, the car crossed over to the other side of the road. Thankfully, there were no cars coming. I could have easily killed all four of us, as well as a family travelling in the opposite direction.

And why did this happen? Expectation. My self-imposed expectation of what my friends wanted prevented me from seeing reason. I created an expectation in my head and didn't let reality (the fact I was about to kill everyone) sway me from my goal of getting back to the hotel.

Expectation is insidious. It is a siren with a silky, seductive, and rational voice that lures you in a direction you may not, on balanced reflection, wish to go. Expectation is something that clouds otherwise good judgement.

I've talked about the benefits of anticipation in brightening up your life. Expectation can be like anticipation, as in, "I'm expecting something good to happen." But I'm not talking about that sort of expectation here. I'm talking about imposed expectation, be it self or external. I'm talking about doing things because you think you should.

People talk about "moral compasses." In any decision-making process, there is the potential to wander in good or bad directions. The moral compass is that little voice that tells you, "This isn't a good idea," or, "Do you really think you should be doing that?" It's the professor in your head we talked about before. I think of the moral compass as being a force drawing you in a moral direction, like a magnet. If we stick with the magnet analogy, expectation is also a force drawing you in one direction or another. Whereas the moral compass is directed by your conscience, expectation is directed by a premise that may or may not be valid. Expectation can drag you off course without you knowing it. I felt a "need" to get my friends back to their hotel. The urgency of that expectation clouded my judgement and almost killed us.

Let's look at another example to explain it better. I think we all agree that everyone should be given the opportunity to pursue their own paths in life. We all want our kids to be happy, and we all want them working at something they enjoy. Now suppose your parents, grandparents, and great-grandparents have been farmers for generations, and you're the only child of the next generation. There's a family farm to run, and you've grown up surrounded by the expectation that you will become a farmer, carrying on the family tradition. How hard is that? How can you decide about your life with that heavy weight of expectation on your shoulders? Now, if you want to be a farmer, fantastic; it's all set up for you. But what if you don't? Will the expectation of others allow you to decide in your own best interest?

We've talked about Cialdini's principle of commitment and consistency before. It's the reason goal-setting works. When you make a commitment, your brain is hardwired to help you keep that commitment. Expectation is the dark side of commitment and consistency. It's following through with the commitment to reach the goal without looking at the big picture, without realizing that following through with the commitment is a bad thing.

I was involved in a surgical demonstration on one of my patients. The surgeon was undertaking a new protocol and I was assisting. Only a few of these procedures had been done in the country at that point, and we had a video audience of about thirty dentists in the next room. Anyway, the operation started going badly (patient in pain, surgical guide not quite right, things going in the wrong direction). There was a strong sense of expectation in the room. All these people had turned up to see this operation performed in a specific manner and it wasn't seemly to bail at the first hurdle. To the surgeon's credit, he did abandon the procedure at an appropriate time and in the patient's best interest, but the pressure of expectation was immense.

If you find yourself in a situation where you're not sure you should be doing something, have a good, hard, detached look at what's happening and see if you are a victim of expectation, be it self-imposed or because of some external pressure.

In the greater scheme of things, you should not create expectations of outcomes that will lead to disappointment if they're not met. You don't want to raise hopes and then dash them. You don't want to promise things you can't deliver. You don't want to put yourself in a position where there is pressure to deliver an outcome that on calmer reflection is not appropriate.

Trans-American Journey Analogy

Expectation is like taking the wrong turn at a fork in the road and then refusing to look at the map. Sometimes you have to pause and look at the big picture to realize that you've committed yourself to a path that isn't going to get you where you want to go, or worse still, will lead you to danger.

in summary

Avoid where possible creating expectations. If you find things aren't going according to plan, pause and look at the big picture. Are you somehow being drawn or pushed in the wrong direction? Have the strength to realize that you're only doing something because of the weight of expectation, not because it's a good idea.

4.9 Complacency

Great. I get to tell another story about how my stupidity almost killed someone. This book is starting to mess with my self-esteem. OK, deep breath, Brett . . . you can get through this.

As you will recall, this book has only been possible because I've analyzed my mistakes and tried to figure out if there was a lesson to be learned. Luckily for you people, I've made a lot of mistakes.

Complacency means "a feeling of quiet pleasure or security, often while unaware of some potential danger." The "someone" I've almost killed (many times) through complacency is me. I'm sorry to say that most of you are probably making the same mistake.

I mentioned earlier the lump in my neck that I ignored for many years that turned out later to be cancer. It didn't hurt. It didn't bother me. It didn't seem to be getting worse, so I ignored it. That is complacency.

I treat patients with dental appliances for sleep apnea. People with untreated sleep apnea are five times more likely to get cancer. I have a home tester, so I tested myself. The results showed that I had moderate sleep apnea. It didn't hurt. It didn't bother me. It didn't seem to be getting worse. So I ignored it.

I had a routine blood test done. It revealed I had high cholesterol. It didn't hurt. It didn't bother me. It didn't seem to be getting worse. So I ignored it.

As I got older I put on a few pounds and stopped exercising. I became very unfit. It didn't hurt. It didn't bother me . . . well, I think you can see a pattern here.

On the surface, complacency doesn't seem as bad as apathy. If you're apathetic, you don't care, and if you're complacent, you're just happy with where you are and what you're doing. I mean at least you're happy; that's got to be a good thing, right?

Let me tell you the greatest lesson my life challenges have revealed to me. It's so important that I'm going to write it in capital letters and give it its own line:

IT DOESN'T' HAPPEN TO YOU
UNTIL IT HAPPENS TO YOU.

It sounds simple enough, but until you've experienced the shock of something totally unexpected happening to you, it's hard to comprehend.

Complacency is thinking it won't happen to you. Most smokers have this bad. They think they'll be the one that beats the odds and lives a long and healthy life. You nonsmokers should not feel so smug. Based on my observations of, oh, let me see . . . *almost everyone*, people usually take their own health for granted.

I've been given a fabulous gift: the inability to take my health for granted. I statistically have a 30 percent chance of living another five years (which may be five years ago by the time you read this). That tends to focus one's attention.

So, what can you learn from my stupidity? How can you fight complacency? First, get serious about your health and get serious now. The most important thing in life is being alive. Everything else falls into second place after that. Take setting your long-term health goals seriously.

I became a vegan because I believe that diet is my best chance of beating cancer (along with a positive attitude). I don't expect everyone to become a vegan, but eating healthy is not rocket science. The closer you approach a whole-food vegan diet, the healthier you will be, so approach it as close as you can. Eat more fresh fruit and vegetables; reduce meat, dairy, and processed foods. Reduce sugar (eliminating it would be better) and reduce all fats and oils. Avoid fast food. Fast food is slow death.

Lose weight and exercise. It's a cliché, but just fucking do it! Excuse my bad language, but overcoming complacency is hard. Also, get checked for sleep apnea. Only 10 percent of people with sleep apnea have been diagnosed. You could easily have it without knowing. It is prevalent but treatable. Remember, as I said earlier, people with untreated sleep apnea are five times more likely to get cancer. I had untreated sleep apnea and I got cancer. Coincidence? Maybe, but it doesn't happen to you until it happens to you.

> If you go to www.simplifyinglife.me
> there will be up-to-date stuff
> you can read on health.

The problem with complacency is that it prevents you from moving forward. When you start getting happy with the status quo of your life, then the journey stops. And I don't think the journey should ever stop. Humans are like sharks: We need to keep moving to stay alive. If you aren't moving mentally, if your life isn't progressing in some direction, then you will stagnate and die, either physically or emotionally.

You can't be complacent with your health. You need to act and act now. In other areas of your life, sure, it may be OK to be complacent for short periods. Let's liken life to running a marathon. The better marathon runners can maintain an even pace the entire race. You may be a great marathon runner, but I'm not. I run as far as I can, then I stop and rest, then I run as far as I can again. I repeat this process until I finish the race (or don't). I think it's OK to take a breather on your journey, to stop and reflect, to pause and reassess, and to rest on your laurels for a while. But I don't think you should do it forever. You can allow yourself the luxury of being complacent for short periods, but if you pause too long in your journey, then what else is there to do? The journey will be over before you know it. Good night, see you later.

Don't get me wrong, I think it's a great thing to be happy with your lot in life. The problem is, I don't think you can stay happy if you're not moving forward. When your health starts to affect you, I'm confident you won't be happy. Complacency is giving up on getting better. It's giving up on your progress.

The whole point of life is the journey (well, at least that's the way I see it). If you're not on the journey, you're not living. Keep moving, keep going forward, keep getting healthier, never be too content, always be a little restless, always want to learn and do a little more.

Trans-American Journey Analogy

Complacency is when your car breaks down in a pleasant town and you don't bother to get it fixed because you've decided to live in this town now.

→ in summary

Take your health seriously and take it seriously now. Eat less meat, dairy, oil, fat, sugar, and fast foods. Eat more fruit and vegetables. Exercise more. We all get tired and need to catch our breath occasionally. But complacency happens when you settle for where you are, and give up on the journey. It may seem like a pleasant short-term solution, but it won't make you as happy as possible. And it won't allow you to live as long as possible. And remember: It doesn't happen to you until it happens to you.

4.10 Comparing Yourself to Others

I think too much about money. Actually, it's not that I think too much about money; it's that I WORRY too much about money. This is stupid, because I live a relatively privileged life. So do you, in fact. If you had enough money to buy this book you're probably better off than the majority of the world's population. I wonder if you ever worry about money, or am I the only one? What is it I worry about and why?

I've got this mate. Let's call him Floyd to simplify things (because his name really is Floyd). Floyd, bless him, is stinking rich. Bill Gates probably doesn't think Floyd's stinking rich, because he's not a billionaire or anything. But you and I would agree that Floyd redefines what it means to be "doing OK." I've got other rich mates, but none quite as rich as Floyd.

He's got a bunch of houses, a bunch of expensive cars, and he travels most places by private jet. I'm sure you get the picture.

Floyd is also one of the nicest, smartest, most generous guys you'd ever want to meet. It is no accident Floyd is rich. He wasn't given his money; he worked hard to get it and he enjoys sharing the largess of his labors. It is very difficult to begrudge Floyd his success.

It is natural to compare yourself to more successful people, to wonder what it would be like to have their lives. It can, however, be a VERY dangerous trap to fall into. If no one was better off than you, then you'd feel on top of the world. But because there ARE people better off than you, then somehow you can feel a little disappointed, like you haven't quite reached your potential. It's still you, but the other people alter your perception of yourself.

I don't envy my rich pals. I don't want their lifestyle or their "stuff." Sure, I enjoy hanging out with them, but I've had just as much fun in a tent as I have in a jet, so I never pretend it's the "stuff" that makes life fun.

The richer that people are, the easier it is for you to NOT compare yourself to them. I can't see myself going from being a suburban dentist to the president of a $1 billion corporation, so it's very easy to ignore them for the purposes of comparison. Because their lives are so different from mine, it's easy not to compare myself to them. When I play golf, I don't get down on myself because I'm not playing like Greg Norman. That would be a ridiculous comparison.

The people who are harder to ignore are your peers. I've got a few friends doing a lot better than me, and I can't help but wonder what I am doing wrong. It's a bad thought to have. I expect I have friends who are not doing as well as me, and I suppose they are thinking, "What am I doing wrong?"

What we're all doing wrong is comparing ourselves to one another. Happiness and unhappiness are relative states of mind. If you are concerned about material wealth, then comparing yourself to others is not going to make you happy (unless you're Bill Gates). You're much better off ignoring everyone else, or pretending there is nothing more you want.

In the context of this aspect of life only, it would be nice if we could live in a vacuum, or at least in blissful ignorance. If you didn't know a better car existed, or if you thought yours was the best car in the world, would you want a different car? The same goes for your house, your clothes, your phone (don't get me started on phones), your TV, your whatever. If you knew nothing better existed, you'd be forced to be content. But being content doesn't keep the advertising people fed. There is an entire industry out there determined to extract your money by making you feel dissatisfied with your life and envious of others. Don't fall for the trap.

So why do I worry about money? It's not because I want Floyd's Ferrari or Bill's beach house (another rich mate). I worry that my family won't be supported if something happens to me. Is it a realistic worry? I hope not, but that's the problem with having kids; all you do is worry, probably because you care so much. I'm trying to put myself in a position where they have a solid financial future, and I'm not there yet. But what if no one was "financially secure"? If "financial security" didn't exist, I wouldn't want it (or know I wanted it). It's only because I compare myself to someone else that I think there is something more I need or want. It is a difficult trap to avoid, and I can't say I have always avoided it, but knowing what the enemy looks like helps you know when he turns up. And then you can be prepared.

Trans-American Journey Analogy

That guy in front of you may have a nicer looking car than yours, but he's still going to end up at the same destination as you. If yours was the only car on the road, then it would be the nicest.

→ ## in summary

You don't covet things that don't exist. Sometimes it feels like other people are better off than you, but that only happens because you compare yourself to them. If you don't compare yourself to anyone else, you will feel a lot more content and happier with your life. Pretend you're the richest person in the world. I bet in many ways you are.

4.10 Distraction

This is something else that has seriously challenged me over the years (and it still does). Without distractions, I would have finished this book five-years ago.

Distraction occurs when urgent things steal time from important things. It is easy to waste time on urgent matters that "have" to get done. Ask any mother with young kids where her time goes. There's always something that "needs" to be done. It isn't hard to fill life with unproductive tasks. I just love how a bill with a due date of today can muscle in on anything else I'm doing.

There's a well-known story that illustrates what I'm getting at. Despite the protestations of my editor, I'm regurgitating the story because I think about this idea all the time. Here's a version I stole from the Internet:

A time-management expert stood in front of a group of high-powered over-achievers and said, 'Okay, time for a quiz.' Then he pulled out a one-gallon, wide-mouthed jar and set it on a table in front of him. Then he produced about a dozen fist-sized rocks and carefully placed them, one at a time, into the jar. When the jar was filled to the top and no more rocks would fit inside, he asked, 'Is this jar full?' Everyone in the class said yes.

Then he reached under the table and pulled out a bucket of gravel. He dumped some gravel in and shook the jar causing pieces of gravel to work themselves down into the spaces between the big rocks. Then he asked the group once more, 'Is the jar full?'

By this time, the class was onto him. 'Probably not,' one of them answered. He reached under the table and brought out a bucket of sand. He started dumping the sand in and it went into all the spaces left between the rocks and the gravel. Once more he asked the question, 'Is this jar full?'

'No!' the class shouted.

Then he grabbed a pitcher of water and began to pour it in until the jar was filled to the brim. Then he looked up at the class and asked, 'What is the point of this illustration?'

One eager beaver raised his hand and said, 'The point is, no matter how full your schedule is, if you try really hard, you can always fit some more things into it!'

'No,' the speaker replied, 'that's not the point. The truth this illustration teaches us is: If you don't put the big rocks in first, you'll never get them in at all.'

This story illustrates why you need written goals and why you need to focus on them daily. Your long-term unrealistic goals are your rocks. You should be visualizing them nightly. If you focus on those goals it is harder to be distracted by the gravel and sand of your life. There will always be enough gravel and sand to fill your life, but the trick is not to let that happen. Figure out how much time you need to achieve your goals and allocate that time first. Let all the other stuff deal with the fact that you ain't movin' your rocks for no one.

If your realistic long-term goal is to get fitter, and that involves walking for thirty minutes a day, then that's a rock. It comes first and everything else finds time around it. If you want to spend more time with your family, then it's a rock. Schedule that time and don't let the background noise of your life encroach on it.

The more you focus on your goals, the less likely you are to be distracted. The moment you lose focus, you'll find yourself covered in sand. Ask me how I know that.

Trans-American Journey Analogy

You ever been distracted driving a car? You ever almost hit something because you were gazing at a pretty girl or hot car or some bloke in a tight T-shirt or whatever rocks your boat? Or have you committed the ultimate sin and replied to a text while driving? (Not smart, people.) Distraction is a disaster waiting to happen. Keep your eyes on the road ahead and stay focused.

in summary

The better you focus on what's important (and you know what that is because you've written it down), the less likely you are to be distracted by urgent demands. Don't let the important things be overwhelmed by the urgent things.

4.11 Lack of Challenges

It is wonderfully ironic that one of life's challenges can be a lack of challenges in life. I just love the fact the universe has a sense humor.

You already know how important I think laughing is. My wife and I have enjoyed introducing our daughters to our favorite comedy movies and television shows as soon as we thought they were old enough to enjoy the humor. I'm very proud to report they have been fans of *Get Smart* from an early age.

At the moment, we're introducing them to *Seinfeld*. Yes, I know not all of the episodes will be age appropriate. Thank God for review sites. While trawling through a review site, I came across the fact that the father of Julia Louis-Dreyfus (who plays Elaine) was a billionaire. He was reported to be worth $3.4 billion in 2006. It is very impressive that Julia has achieved such acclaim despite her upbringing. It's tempting to think that having the world at your feet is a good thing. But I would argue otherwise.

It is a great challenge for successful people to create an environment where their children will be challenged to achieve success. When you start with nothing, if you're the motivated type, the desire to become successful will keep you going. When you come from an environment of privilege (where you want for nothing), finding motivation can be difficult.

There's a biblical saying, "Idle hands are the devil's workshop," which sums it up. Too much money and too much time combined create trouble. The generation that makes the money seems to be motivated to keep making money, and so they don't succumb to the problem. They're focused on continuing to achieve, so they never have too much time. The generation that inherits the money doesn't have the same motivation.

The most famous example of this problem is the Kennedy family. Joseph P. Kennedy Sr. (father of JFK) made a fortune in the first half of the twentieth century, which he put into trusts. The idea would be that his heirs wouldn't have to work. The trust would support their needs and they could go out and do good in the world. The public record would indicate the idea hasn't worked as well as old Joe would have liked.

Bill Gates, the world's richest man understands the problem. He has vowed to donate his fortune (which is approaching $100 billion at the moment) to charity rather than leave it to his kids. Gates said: "Our kids will receive a great education and some money so they are never going to be poorly off but they'll go out and have their own career." He then goes on to make my point with more authority and experience than I can make it: "It's not a favor to kids to have them have huge sums of wealth. It distorts anything they might do, creating their own path."

Well said, Bill. You don't have to be Bill Gates, however, to screw up your kids with too much money. You can achieve the same result with a middle-class income. How many kids do you know who want for nothing? What are you teaching your kids if you give them everything they want? There might not be enough money for boats and jets, but there might be enough pocket money for drugs. In many respects, poorer people are giving their kids a better start in life. They are giving them the gift of being challenged from an early age.

The challenge of being challenged is not just about money, however. Money is a simple marker of success, but the issue is not that simple. Yes, you can be born into wealth and achieve great things. Not all of the Kennedys have screwed up. Julie Louis-Dreyfus has done very well.

Let's go back to the beginning. What was your first big challenge in life? I'd venture to suggest it was learning to walk. Your parents will clearly remember the look of pride, joy, and triumph on your face the first time you took a few steps. A child's first unassisted steps are just that: unassisted.

What was your next big challenge? For me it was making friends when I started school. No one can help you make friends. You have to figure it out for yourself. Having a friend is its own reward.

And on and on it goes. A challenge presents itself, you overcome it, you feel good. Overcoming adversity feels good. Struggling to achieve something feels good. Stretching yourself feels good.

I mentioned early in the book that my famous uncle, Ron Taylor, told me the most fun he had in life was struggling to achieve his dream. Actually, achieving it wasn't as much fun as trying to achieve it. (It's all about the journey, people).

As you make your way through life, you will be challenged (assuming your parents don't hand everything to you on a platter). Challenged to do well at school, challenged to get through college or university, challenged to find a job, challenged to find a mate, challenged to do better in your job, challenged to find meaning and purpose in life.

It's the last one (meaning and purpose) where people can go astray. And it's for that reason you need goals that are unattainable. How can you not be challenged if you are trying to achieve the impossible?

Life HAS to be a challenge. EVERY LITTLE BIT OF IT. I can't make that point strongly enough. You need to be a proverbial mouse finding its way out of the maze. At every step in your life you NEED barriers. Don't complain about the barriers, embrace them.

When life stops being challenging, you stagnate. Are you in a job that doesn't challenge you? Just turn up, do something easy for eight hours, then go home? How does that feel? It doesn't have to be like that. You can find challenges in everything you do, even a menial talk. You can try to do it faster, you can try to do it better, you can try to do it different. The key is to try. If you are trying, you are being challenged.

I can thank a good friend and mentor of mine, Omer Reed, for helping me understand this concept. It was Omer's lifeogy I wrote earlier in the book. Omer, and his wife Marci, are amazing people. Omer is a dental educator, but it's how he educates that sets him apart. You see, he makes you think. He doesn't spoon feed you, he makes you struggle to understand. And it is in the struggle that you find the gift of his knowledge.

Omer believes strongly in the power and the value of the struggle, of being challenged. Omer and Marci's struggle, however, has been greater than most. They had five children, and sadly, four of them have died. They had a daughter die of a brain hemorrhage in her late teens, and three sons have died of cancer in successive decades. They have one surviving daughter.

You wouldn't wish such tragedy on anyone. Omer and Marci have, however, found great strength through adversity (buoyed I'm sure by their strong faith). Their challenges, which I think we can all agree have been greater than most, have made and defined them. One of my earlier concepts is to be an inspiration. The way they have faced and overcome their challenges makes them very inspiring people. They've certainly inspired me, and helped me understand the importance of being challenged.

If your goals are set correctly, then your life will automatically be a challenge. You don't want every moment of every day to be a challenge, but you need enough challenges so that you have the constant satisfaction of overcoming them. If you embrace life as a journey, then you will instinctively know that challenges are what make the journey satisfying.

Trans-American Journey Analogy

If the road was dead straight and flat from Los Angeles to New York, how much fun would the drive be? You need a few curves and hills to make it interesting. You need to break down every now and then to appreciate the kindness of others.

→ in summary

If you're not challenged, you're not going anywhere in life. Set your goals correctly and you will always be challenged. The solution is as simple as that.

Section 5

Strategies
(Advanced Driver Training)

So how are things going? You and I never seem to get time to sit down and chat these days. Well, we're on the home stretch now. I'm very proud of you for sticking it out this far. Organizing your life is not for the faint-hearted, and you're to be congratulated for giving it a go. I know it's a lot easier to just sit around watching TV, which is what I'll probably do when all this is over (just kidding). Seriously, this is a big job, and just having a go will make you feel much better. Sure, I'm trying to make this as easy as possible, but don't feel bad if it's not all coming together yet. Give it a chance, you'll get there.

We've covered a lot of ideas in this chapter before, so you already have a little background knowledge. The point of this section is to give you specific strategies for making the information I've given you so far work better and easier.

If you can drive a car, you can cross the country; but if you have more ability and a few tricks up your sleeve, the trip will be easier, safer, and faster.

"So, what are the tricks, Brett?"

I'm glad you asked.

5.1 Prioritize Tasks

There are lots of good books on time management and this isn't one of them. In fact, every time I come back to this chapter, I change something, so let's not consider me to be the expert on this stuff, OK? I'll tell you what I do, and what my theories are, but if you find a better way, you can drop my techniques like you would a spider sandwich and there will be no hard feelings.

First things first: Figure out what you need to do to achieve your realistic long-term goals and save time for those. Go back to your long-term goals now and decide how much of your week you need to devote to achieving them and when you will work on them.

So, in my case, with writing the book, I saved three hours on Sunday mornings to write the first draft, and now I spend forty-five minutes first thing in the morning Monday to Friday rewriting the second draft. For exercise, I ride my mountain bike for two or three hours early on a Sunday morning before the family stirs, and I go to the gym for an hour on Wednesdays and Saturdays. Those are my rocks that need to be in place for me to achieve my career and health goals.

Do you have YOUR rocks in place? If not, go to your goals and write them down, and then find a place to put your rocks. Life is not a dress rehearsal. It's a one-act play that you only get to act in once.

Your rocks are concreted into place and they will now start to take care of themselves, provided you honor the time you allocated to them. As an aside, focusing on them each night will help you honor them. So, how do we deal with the gravel, sand, and water?

I love eliminating things. When I get a big pile of mail, I hover over the garbage figuring out what I can toss straight away. I'm always trying to simplify my life, and the things I don't need have to go. I act on whatever mail is left. Happiness is an empty inbox. You know what's important; you should focus on that and ignore everything else. I want your mind figuratively perched over the garbage ready to throw out things that need throwing out.

There is, however, a lot of gravel, sand, and water in life to deal with. I'd love to ignore paying the bills because they're not part of the big picture; they do, however, form an important part of the smaller picture, particularly if you want the power to stay connected. So, given the fact that all of the little things still need to be done, what's an efficient way of dealing with them?

At the moment, I'm in love with a task-management program called Nozbe. It's the home page on my desktop and laptop browser, and it's an app on my smart phone. Everything I need to do is written down in Nozbe. If the task has a deadline I give it a deadline. Nothing is forgotten. It is where all my sand and gravel lives.

I subscribe to the theory that if you write everything down, it reduces your stress levels. As much as possible, I try NOT to put myself in a position where I HAVE to remember things. That adds stress in my life that I don't need. My nirvana is to have everything I need to do in a prioritized list. I like my life to be organized, as much as possible, like a pilot's checklist. Commercial airline pilots don't make things up. Best practice has been determined, and they follow best practice in an orderly step-by-step manner. That's how I'd like my life to be. It is, to be honest, a work in progress, but I can see myself getting there with the help of Nozbe.

There is also a great book called *The Checklist Manifesto* that explains the value of checklists and it's worth a read. The key is to write things down and to have a system.

Trans-American Journey Analogy

If you pull up to a gas station, almost on empty, hungry, and busting to use the bathroom, you'll know how to prioritize the tasks.

⟶ **in summary**

Make sure everything you need to do is written down somewhere. Look at your long-term goals and set aside time to work on them. These are your rocks, and time for them is sacred. Manage your gravel, sand, and water in the time remaining.

5.2 Problem Solving

So, we've established that I love writing things down. There are a couple of reasons for that. First, if it's written down it doesn't get forgotten, and second, if it's written down it doesn't seem so onerous. In the previous chapter, we wrote down all our tasks. In this chapter, we write down all the problems.

I like to think of a problem as an issue for which the solution is not readily apparent. It's an impasse, a barrier beyond which you may or may not see a solution.

The very perceptive among you will be thinking: "But Brett, if I've set my goals correctly and cast my vision beyond the horizon, these problems you speak of are mere trifles of minimal consequence. Bother me not with them." You would of course be correct. But in deference to the one-in-a-million person out there in reader-land who may have a residual problem lurking in the dim, dark recesses of a sullied subconscious, we will, out of mere academic curiosity, look at a way of solving them. You may have a friend who needs your help and who hasn't read the book, so let's read on with an open mind.

Do you ever feel like you're an expert at solving other people's problems, but an amateur at solving your own? Maybe it's just a boy thing. We boys love *solving* problems, whereas you girls love *sharing* problems. It's a weird division of responsibilities, if you ask me. Someone certainly had a sense of humor when they made men and women so different.

Maybe I should explain this for all of you who have no idea what I'm talking about. I got this concept about men and women from the book, *Men Are from Mars, Women Are from Venus*. In simple terms, men exchange information whereas women exchange emotions. So, if you go to a typical Australian party where men congregate around the BBQ, you will hear all the blokes talking about "stuff." We talk about cars, we talk about news, we talk about sports. We exchange facts, we talk about things that are real, and things you can touch.

If perchance the women are out of earshot, and we've had a bit too much to drink, you may actually chance upon a group of men accidentally discussing a problem. Your average Aussie bloke will not be too comfortable with this situation, however. You can't show weakness when you're a man, except in a self-deprecating way, which is really a show of strength, as in: "Look at me; I've got this problem and I don't care." So, discussing a problem is going to make the other men feel uncomfortable. We don't like stumbling into emotional territory. So, to avoid discussing the problem we'll attempt to fix it as quickly as possible.

I'll give you an example. When I'm out with Roddy and Michael, we talk about cars. We'll do that for five or six hours. Occasionally, we'll run out of car things to discuss. In those cases, we venture into sports. I'm not a big fan of football, so if they steer the conversation that way, I steer it toward golf (my special subject). They don't know much about golf, so we might change direction and talk about wine, boats, property prices, or holiday destinations—all areas of common interest. We focus on facts and information with a few unsubstantiated opinions thrown in. Now that I think about it, in the twenty years or more that I've know them, we've never discussed an emotion or feeling. So, I'll make one up. I might say something like, "I'm worried about the amount of debt I've got. If interest rates go much higher I'm screwed." If I said that, I can guarantee that they'd both go into problem-solving mode, using questions such as: How much debt have you got? What interest rates are you paying? What rental returns are you getting? What are they worth if you dump them? Give a man a problem and he'll try to fix it.

Women, on the other hand, exchange emotions. When Donna, Liz, and Kerry talk, they look for common ground to empathize with one another. If they talk about the kids, they look for consensus. A typical question is: "Did you have the same problems as me?"

This is not problem-solving, it's problem-sharing. The solution is not the goal; it's the sharing of the problem that is the goal. They're happy to accept advice, but the empathy is more important than the solution. And we boys don't really get that.

So, a typical miscommunication at our house would involve me getting home from work and asking Donna how her day was and being told about an incident that had brought her to the brink of infanticide followed by me analyzing what happened and offering suggestions on handling the situation better in the future. Yep, that sort of approach will push her to the brink of husbandicide.

What I should always do is summon the strength to fight my natural male urges and listen intently, to sympathize with her plight, to never suggest how to solve the problem.

The point I'm trying to make is that everyone else's problems seem so easy to fix, but for some reason our own problems can seem insurmountable. If you took your problems to your average bloke, they'd have a plan for fixing them in a jiffy. Your average woman would empathize for a while before getting to the advice bit. Most people would be happy to have a stab at solving your problems, just as you would do for them. Well, return the favor to yourself.

I want you to pretend that your problems are someone else's. Write them down. Do it now. What are the three biggest problems in your life at this moment? Write them down now and *don't even think* about reading on until you've written something down. This is a learning exercise and you won't learn if you don't participate. I don't care what you write, just write something. I'll give you mine:

1. Stress from owing too much money

2. Not spending enough time with the kids

3. Too many projects need to be completed

Write yours here:

1. _____

2. _____

3. _____

OK, now imagine that a good friend comes up to you with exactly the same problem. Say it out loud if your imagination is challenged. What are you going to say? What's your solution? What's your advice? Do you see what's happened? You've now got someone about as smart as you helping you solve your problems. If you're a person who has an opinion about other people's problems, you should be able to use this technique to overcome a few of your own hurdles in life.

Now, this is easy for me to say because I'm one of those people (hence the book). If you aren't a person who is good at solving problems or offering advice, then this technique is probably not for you. Give it a go, but don't beat yourself up if it isn't working.

Deep down most of us know the answers to our problems. The trick is to get outside yourself. Sometimes you can't see the forest for the trees. Well, sometimes you can't appreciate the problem because you're in the middle of the problem. If you write it down and think of it as someone else's problem, it's a little less personal and the answer is a little more obvious. Stepping back helps you to provide your own objective opinion. It helps to have a history of talking to yourself like I do. Glad I never took that medication. Where would I be now?

The more you think about a problem (with a blank sheet of paper and pen in hand) the clearer the solution becomes. Try it.

Trans-American Journey Analogy

On a long trip, there's a good chance that you'll have a mechanical problem. You can either sit on the side of the road feeling sorry for yourself, or you can logically look at possible solutions to your problem.

➤ in summary

Write your problems down and try to solve them as if they were someone else's problems. Give yourself the advice you would give to someone in exactly the same situation. If you have the answers for other people, then they're inside waiting to help you. Don't waste or ignore your own potential to help yourself.

5.3 Did I Look at the Worst-Case Scenario?

This is a simple strategy for helping you make decisions. People who are used to making decisions know that *no* decision is generally worse than a *bad* decision, but this point is lost on many people.

If you have trouble making a decision about anything, run through this little protocol. Think about the decision you have to make, and then consider the absolute worst repercussion of making the absolute worst decision. What you will probably discover is that we often worry about things that really don't matter. I'm hoping this little process will help you realize that.

I often ask my wife which shirt goes with which pants. The truth of the matter is that it almost never matters. If we're going out with friends, they don't care how I look. If I get close to the right decision, it will be fine; and if I make the world's worst fashion decision, will it make any difference?

What decisions trouble you? Which ones do you find hard to make? I wasn't sure which university course I wanted to take. I did my research on schools, but I still wasn't sure. It was a decision I labored over before I decided on dentistry. What if it had been the wrong decision? Choosing a career is a big decision. If I'd applied my "what is the worst-case scenario test," I would have realized that even a bad decision would have worked out fine. I would have known within the first year that dentistry wasn't for me, and then I could have transferred to another course, probably with credit for what I'd done. Not life or death, is it?

What if it is life or death? Yes, there are lots of decisions out there that are critical, and we should worry about those. For all the rest, take a hard look at the possible repercussions of a wrong decision, and I think you will be pleasantly surprised that most things really don't matter. Worry about what you should worry about, not the rest.

Another approach is to look at the consequences of a decision in the context of time. If you get a decision wrong, will it matter tomorrow? Will it matter next week or next month? What about next year, or in ten or twenty years? When you're able to put things in a time perspective, you often find you are wasting emotional energy on things that will be irrelevant or forgotten within a short period of time. Climate change? Sure, worry about that. It could be a problem for centuries. Whether to have the cabernet or the shiraz with your pasta? Worst-case scenario is that it's a problem for an hour. Let's not worry about that.

Trans-American Journey Analogy

Taking the wrong turn isn't the end of the world. You'll end up in the right place eventually. There are very few wrong turns you can't recover from.

> ➡ **in summary**
>
> If you are having trouble making a decision, look at the worst-case scenario of making a wrong decision. Knowing how important a decision really is (when put in the correct context) will help you make it and move on.

5.4 Am I Being True to Myself?

This is your all-purpose decision-making tool. You should be asking yourself this question most of the time. If you compromise your integrity, you make life harder for yourself. When decisions you make (or actions you take) reflect your values, your world is in sync. It feels right. If you start to wander off course, straying from who you really are and what you believe, life gets harder and less simple. And we don't approve of that sort of thing around here, do we?

Let me give you an example. I live on a river. I'm good when it comes to pollution. I would never think of throwing a Styrofoam cup or a plastic bottle or anything that wasn't biodegradable into the river. I do, however, throw things in that I think the fish will eat (bits of meat and bread). My "grey area" in the river pollution issue is related to things that will rust away. I have been known to throw a rusty nail (not complete car bodies) into the river. I rationalize the act because I know they will eventually rust away.

I'm sure everyone out there in reader-land is absolutely riveted by my pangs of conscience in matters of the environment, but I'm trying to make a point. The truth is, now that I think about it, I'm not actually comfortable throwing anything in the river, even something that will rust away to nothing. I'm not being true to myself doing that. It isn't really ME, if you know what I mean. I'm better than that (or at least I think I am). Not being true to ME is a stress in my life I don't need.

My neighbor's son was skipping stones on the water one day. He wanted the beer bottle tops I had in my pocket. (I have no idea how they got there; maybe the beer fairies left them.) I was about to give them to him (rationalizing they would rust away) when I noticed there was a plastic insert in the bottle top. Throwing plastic in the river was crossing the line for me, so I didn't give them to him. I wouldn't have been true to myself. I sent him scavenging for flat rocks instead.

We discussed the professor (your conscience) earlier. The professor knows you better than anyone else, and has most (if not all) of the answers to the problems and challenges in your life. It's a tremendous resource few people draw upon. You see, everyone intuitively knows what is right for them. You may say you don't know, but you know. There's a little voice inside your head. You can try to ignore it, but you can't turn it off. That little voice cannot be quieted.

People often ask me what they should do about their personal issues. I invariable say, "What do you think you should do?" They invariably know. The answers are in your head people. Listen to them. Listen to the voices.

Do you have any difficult decisions to make? Take a few moments and ask yourself: "Am I being true to myself?" What was the answer? It's there. It has to be there. Now assume for a moment that you accept that answer. How do you feel? If it's the right answer, you probably feel calm.

Too many of us spend too much time fighting ourselves. That voice in our heads knows the direction our life should take. Think of that voice as the worst possible TV caricature of a nagging spouse (hair in a bun, apron, rolling pin in hand—you know the type) telling you everything you're doing wrong. Well, that's the voice you hear when you ignore your conscience. You can't fight your conscience forever. It's too hard.

When you are true to yourself, when you are true to your own values, you experience an incredible calm. Just don't fight it. This is one example of where the path of least resistance is the correct path.

Have you ever experienced that wonderful sensation you get when you have done the right thing? I'm an imperfect person now, but I've been more imperfect in the past. I used to be a person who would keep the money if someone gave me too much change in a store. Sure, I'd have more money, but I wouldn't feel good about myself. Now I always give the money back and I always get this sense of calm. I check the bill at restaurants in case they've forgotten to charge me for something. Every time I do the right thing I get this fantastic calm feeling. My mind is obviously rewarding me for being a good boy. Being true to my own values is the path of least resistance, the path of pleasure.

I was recently at a winery in the Napa Valley in California. It was one of those places where you had to pay to taste the wine. It was very busy and our server said he would charge us at the end. He went missing half way through, so another lady completed our tasting. I asked to pay when she gave me the last glass of wine and she said, "You've already paid." I said, "No I haven't." She said, "You're supposed to pay at the beginning." I said, "But I didn't. It's a karma thing. I have to pay." She thanked me for being honest, told me I could have easily walked out without paying (I knew that), and poured me a couple of extra glasses of wine to reward me. She then asked me for the wrong amount. I said, "No, that's not right. We had the premium wines, you should be charging me more than that." She said, "You know what, I'm not charging anything, it's a karma thing." I could have insisted on paying, but I could tell she felt good about making that decision, so I didn't.

That's the universe rewarding me for doing the right thing. I could have walked out and gypped "the man." (It was a large faceless corporate winery, not a mom and pop operation.) But I wouldn't have felt right doing that. I didn't even feel right about not paying, so I bought a nice bottle on the way out with the money I saved, so at least they got a little money out of me. At that point my conscience was clear.

Trans-American Journey Analogy

If you feel guilty speeding, then don't do it.

in summary

Everyone intuitively knows what is right for them. That little voice cannot be quieted. When you are true to yourself you will experience a calm that confirms you chose the correct path.

5.5 Have I Learned the Lessons?

Life is constantly trying to teach you lessons. The smarter you are, the quicker you learn them. What's the point of having something go wrong if you don't learn from it?

I know this idiot dentist. I won't even allude to his name because he'll sue me. I try to see the positive in most people, but I've given up on this guy. He's pretty smart, but he is in no way, shape, or form introspective. This guy has a small business, but he has had hundreds of different staff members over the years because none of them stay very long (he fires them or they resign). He thinks all of them are useless. He says none of them listen to him and that none of them are motivated in their jobs.

Now if it was me, after maybe the first thirty or forty had quit, I'd be wondering if maybe I was the problem, and NOT the staff members. This level of insight hasn't yet dawned on Dr. Blame-the-World.

My point is, if the same thing keeps going wrong, then look for other answers. Early in the book, I said I like to assume first that I'm the problem. Don't be afraid of embracing this approach. It should bring you comfort to know YOU are the problem, because then you have complete control over fixing it.

I've got a few friends who have been married several times. They seem to make all the mistakes in the second marriage that they made in the first. Slow learners. It doesn't matter what the situation is, when something goes wrong, try to figure out what happened. Don't repeat the mistake. What is the lesson to be learned? Have you learned it? If you think all the mistakes and problems in your life are due to some pernicious outside influence, then you are missing the lesson. Look at every problem as an opportunity to learn. The old line that you only learn from your mistakes is a truism we should all embrace a little more enthusiastically.

I still make lots of mistakes, and I still have trouble learning all the lessons. I guess that's part of the journey. I keep trying though.

Trans-American Journey Analogy

There's a hamburger chain I only eat at when I'm driving, and I always feel sick afterwards. I've really got to learn that lesson.

in summary

When things aren't going right, have a good, hard look at the situation and figure out the lesson to be learned. Try to learn it and don't repeat the mistake.

5.6 Apologize and Move On

We all have a vested interest in being right. To function in life, you need to have confidence in your decisions or nothing gets done. Will I buy the red shirt or the blue shirt? Whatever decision you make, you will have a reason for making that decision, and you could use that reason to defend your decision in an argument.

Too many people spend too much time in life engaged in petty arguments defending their positions. They think being right is important. It's not, and the sooner you figure that out, the happier your life will be. You will be wrong a lot of the time, and that's nothing to worry about. Just don't fall into the trap of always thinking you're right, because it will disrupt your life.

Let's go back to our journey analogy. Your life is like driving from one side of the US to the other. Let's imagine that you've got a super-efficient car, and you've got a full tank of gas, enough to last the entire journey. Pretend that tank of gas HAS to last the entire journey. You can't fill up, there's nothing extra, it's just enough to get you there. If you run out of steam (I love mixing metaphors) then you're not going to make it.

So, the smart thing would be to not lose momentum on your journey. The smart thing would be to not stop unnecessarily. The smart thing would be to not get sidetracked or detoured.

Arguments are one of life's greatest energy burners and time wasters. We all get into disputes that go nowhere. Just apologize and move on. It really doesn't matter who's right or wrong. If you are constantly held up by petty arguments, you are wasting energy that you desperately need to complete your journey.

It is too easy, when you're involved in a dispute, to paint yourself into a corner and waste time and energy trying to talk yourself out of it. Don't bother. Apologize and move on.

Email and social media have become great ways to waste time and energy on arguments. I inevitably get sucked into pointless arguments that don't seem pointless when I start, but soon descend into pointlessness. Give it up. I apologize even when I'm sure I'm right. I don't need the aggravation.

The power of apology is one of life's great secrets. I'm amazed people don't use it more often. It will almost always get you out of trouble and make you feel and look good. Apologies result in a win-win situation. Find someone close to you now and apologize about anything. Here's a couple of ideas:

1. **To spouse:** "I'm sorry, honey. I've been taking you for granted lately. I really do appreciate everything you do for me."

2. **To boss:** "I apologize for not being as efficient as I could. I know you put a lot of trust in me and I want to repay it."

3. **To employee:** "I apologize for taking your hard work for granted. I get so caught up in my own work that I forget to compliment the great work being done by those around me."

4. **To kids:** "I apologize for always mentioning the things you do wrong. I should spend more time mentioning all the things you do right."

That's just a few ideas. Look around and find anything to apologize for. Any minor indiscretion will do. Just apologize for it and see how good it feels and how good the other person feels.

Trans-American Journey Analogy

How angry do you get when another driver does something stupid that almost causes you to have an accident? How do you feel if they immediately give you "the sorry wave"? You know the one. It takes the heat out of the situation, doesn't it? If you don't get an acknowledgement, if you don't get an apologetic wave, how angry do you feel then?

→ # in summary

If an argument or dispute has made you pause on your journey, then just apologize and move on. It is unlikely that the dispute is worth the delay. Even if you are right, apologize and move on. Apology is a very powerful and underused interpersonal skill. Don't be fooled into thinking you're always right. You won't be. I'm sorry I have to be the one to tell you that. Please forgive me.

5.7 Compartmentalize Your Problems

It would be nice if we could make every bit of our lives perfect. It would also be nice if I could be skinny without watching what I eat and exercising. Neither of those things are going to happen. No matter how well we plan our lives, things are going to go wrong. But in the greater scheme of things, what goes wrong is going to make our lives better; it just won't seem like that at the time. The problems, when they occur, are going to seem like problems. So, what do we do?

Well, we don't let a few problems spread and infect every corner of our world. At the end of your life, with the benefit of hindsight and per-spective, most problems will seem trivial. A problem you have overcome is always trivial later. When you are in the middle of a problem, it will seem like a big deal. No amount of rationalization is going to completely eliminate that. The trick is to compartmentalize the problem.

The classic example of this is the balance between work and home. If you have a stressful job, then as much as possible leave that job at work. Don't infect your family life with the problems of your work life.

It works in reverse, too. Don't sabotage your job if your family life is not going great. Try to pigeonhole your problems and not let them expand to occupy the entirety of your life.

I've got all sorts of daily work challenges. A business needs constant tweaking and improving. It is a process that never ends. I have patients all the time that don't get better as quick as I'd like, or they hurt when they shouldn't hurt. Are these the sorts of things my kids need to know about? Should my family be adversely affected by what happens at work? Of course not. My work problems should stay at work when I walk out the office door at night. They'll still be there when I walk in the door the next morning.

I've also had a few financial challenges over the years. Should I worry about them all the time? Will worrying about them make them better? Sure, I need to take them seriously, and sure, I need to do my best to fix them, but I can't let them affect the rest of my life.

Be mindful, however, that there is a big difference between a real problem and an imagined problem. Real problems remain problems until solved. Imagined problems are things you worry about in anticipation of them (maybe) occurring.

As I explained earlier, I've always had a dodgy heart. Let me give you more detail about that. The problem was identified and diagnosed when I was nineteen. When I was twenty-three, it became necessary to correct the problem. That involved cutting my chest open through my left side, slicing out a section of my aorta, and sewing in some Teflon. I don't know if you've ever had your chest cut open, but it's not as fun as it sounds. I was told I'd need another operation in my forties or fifties. So, what did I do after the first operation? Worry every day about something in the distant future I had no control over? Or compartmentalize that problem and worry about it when it needed worrying about?

At age forty-six, I had the second operation and it wasn't a lot of fun either, but worrying about it for twenty-three years wasn't going to make it more fun. Worrying means you get to suffer twice. You suffer in an anticipation of the problem, and then you get to suffer all over again when the problem actually eventuates. If it never happens you get to suffer once for nothing.

My current potential for worry has to do with the cancer in my neck. I was forty-nine when they cut the tumor out from under my jaw, but they didn't get all of it. I had to have radiotherapy to my neck to try to kill any tumor cells that had spread. The radiation dose they give you is the equivalent of six hundred years of background radiation, or two hundred chest CT scans . . . a day! . . . for six weeks! It's not as fun as it sounds.

Anyway, the oncologist won't give me a clean bill of health. They scan me every two years looking to see if it's spread. Do I worry about it constantly between scans? No. What's the point? Sure, I get nervous waiting for the results after the scan, but I don't let it dominate the rest of my life. I compartmentalize it.

So, try not to worry unnecessarily. If you must worry, only worry about real problems, not potential problems, and don't let problems in one part of your life dominate the other parts of your life. That's not playing fair to the bits of your life that are doing fine.

Trans-American Journey Analogy

If you get a scratch on your new car, don't let it burn you up. The rest of the car is still fine.

➤ in summary

Worrying about a problem doesn't make it go away. Your life has many facets (work, spouse, kids, family, friends, health, finance, community), and if one part of the big picture isn't exactly how you'd like it to be, then don't let it spoil the rest of your life. Just because dessert is no good doesn't mean the rest of the meal wasn't great.

5.8 Autopilot Solutions to Problems

In general terms, there are two sorts of lives: the ones that are too busy, and the ones that aren't busy enough. This book is aimed at people like me (and most of my friends) who fall into the former category (too busy). If you're not too busy, good for you. Pop off to the bathroom and give your teeth a good flossing. If you are too busy, you probably want to be less busy. A simple way to be less busy is to put your life on autopilot whenever possible. By that I mean take advantage of whatever modern techniques are available to simplify mundane tasks.

For instance, I have to pay 104 personal bills each year related to things like phones, Internet, electricity, municipal taxes, credit cards, etc. Most of these bills can be paid automatically. I've got to pay them, so why waste time thinking about them? If you take the time to set up automatic payments from your bank account or credit card, you don't have to clutter your life (and your mind) with the burden of paying them. There is also a small but not insignificant level of stress associated with an unpaid bill. Some small part of the engine that is your mind has to worry about that bill until it's paid. Give your mind a break and make sure it doesn't have to worry about trivial stuff.

Shopping these days can also be put on autopilot. When our kids were younger, my wife would shop for groceries online. If you've ever been shopping with toddlers, then you'll know what a challenge it is. If you've never done that, borrow a couple of fully grown goats and take them to the local supermarket. That'll give you an insight into what it's like. Anyway, shopping with children and/or goats is not a significant source of relaxation; so, if you want to save yourself several hours, and many grey hairs, consider online shopping.

Of course, it can be fun to shop, and if you enjoy it, don't let me stop you. I love popping up to my local hardware store to chat with Kevin. Even if I could get it cheaper and quicker somewhere else, I wouldn't. But when a task becomes a chore, or prevents me from doing something more enjoyable, that's when I take the autopilot option if it's available. You should, too.

Trans-American Journey Analogy

If you've got the option of cruise control, use it. (That was too easy.)

→ in summary

If you have the option of automating a task in your life (like paying bills or shopping), and it will save you time, then do it.

5.9 Make the Hard Decisions (the Ones that Matter) Now

This quote is widely attributed to Albert Einstein: "The most powerful force in the universe is compound interest." Sadly, my good friends at snopes.com think the quote is probably bullshit. This is not to say that compound interest is unimpressive; indeed, if Albert were around to ask, he'd probably profess some level of admiration.

Do you ever think you should invest for the future? Put money away for your retirement? It wasn't much of a priority for me when I was young, and it wasn't much of a priority when I was older. In fact, the whole saving and investing thing was something I put on the backburner for years because it was too hard. But there's the issue: Sometimes the things that are "too hard" are the things that need to be done now.

Saving and investing is a great example. It's a hard decision to make and easily delayed. I mean if you don't save this year you can always save next year, right? Of course, you can; but you get less compound interest, which may or may not have impressed Albert, but it sure impresses me. Let's see if I can impress you.

Imagine that you had a rich great, great, great, uncle Talbot who left $1,000 in a bank account 150 years ago and it sat there earning a lousy 5 percent interest. What does compound interest do to $1,000? It turns it into $1.78 million in 150 years, that's what it does. Pretty amazing, isn't it? Imagine if he only left $100 but it earned 8 percent interest. That would turn into $15.64 million. If, however, that $100 was earning 11 percent a year, it would turn into $1.36 billion. That's billion with a B. Now if that doesn't impress you, then I'm giving up.

It's hard for most of us to conjure up a long-lost uncle with an overlooked bank account, so let me give you a more realistic example. Suppose your grandfather gave you $10,000 when you were ten years old and showed you how to invest it wisely for your retirement. You managed to get a 15 percent annual return on your money from age ten to age sixty-five. Without ever adding a cent of your own money, compound interest would turn that $10,000 into $36,358,136.23. Now my fancy math is conveniently ignoring government taxes and bank charges, but they couldn't take all of the $36 million, could they? Yes, you're right; they probably could, but let's pretend for a while that they don't.

Compound interest relies on time. The longer the time available, the higher the return can be. My point is that you need to start saving early. It's a hard decision to make, but it's the hard decisions that often bring you the greatest long-term gain.

Where they take your money is with credit card interest, and they take it big time. If you're a person who only pays the minimum payment on credit cards, you are probably being royally screwed. It's very easy to just go with the status quo, but it will pay you to look around and see if you can transfer your money to a different credit card with lower interest rates. This is another of those hard decisions because it's a real pain to do. You're probably thinking it's only a few percentage points, so what's it going to matter? Well, just as your money can increase rapidly with a few extra percentage points, so your debts can multiply with a few percentage points. This is a hard decision that will potentially save you a lot of money, so make it now. Don't put it off.

Health care can also involve hard decisions. It's easy when you're young to take your health for granted. A little bit of smoking, a little bit of drinking, a few extra pounds, eating improperly, not enough exercise, maybe a few drugs along the way (legal and illegal)—you can get away with a few mistakes when you're in your twenties or thirties, but what about later? A pack-a-day smoker functions fine at age twenty-five, but what about at sixty-five? A fat thirty-year-old isn't likely to have a heart attack, but a fat fifty-year-old might.

Just as compound interest makes your money multiply as you get older, bad health decisions multiply your risk of problems as you get older. The sooner you start saving, the richer you get; the sooner you take your health seriously the healthier you'll stay. But it's a hard decision to make.

People tend to ignore these hard decisions because they can be delayed, but I think you need to confront them now. Take the time to consider the consequences of not making a decision. There are plenty of other decisions you can make in life, but I would contend that you need to set aside some time to address the hard decisions, the ones you want to ignore or delay.

But it's not just money or health; there are many other areas of life where you will dodge a hard decision because you can. Suppose you know your marriage isn't working. It functions maybe, but it isn't as good as it could be, or you've stayed together just for the kids. You must decide to make the relationship better or move on. It's a VERY hard decision to make, so you just put up with the situation and tread water. Years can go by while you delay the decision. Your life can go by while you delay a decision.

What about your job or career? Many people put up with unsatisfying careers because their job is OK, but not great. They make no decision and stay in a job that isn't fulfilling, or isn't working, or isn't fun. Changing jobs, changing careers, these are hard decisions to make. It's much easier to maintain the status quo and put up with things the way they are. You can waste your life by ducking an important decision.

I run a small business and have contact with lots of people who run small businesses. We all employ people, and not all of them are stars. A constant theme on my email chat groups is what to do with under-performing employees. What we as employers do is to put up with average or poor performance because it's too hard to motivate the employee or too hard to fire them. We dodge the hard decisions and go for years not enjoying our jobs because of the people we surround ourselves with. You put up with things because the decision to move an employee along is too hard. When that employee finally leaves, you realize how disruptive they were, and how much better you and everyone else feels now that they're gone. So why didn't you fire them years ago? Because it was a hard decision that could be avoided.

What I want you to do now is to face your hard decisions and do something about them. Select one related to finances, health, relationships, or career. Pick one now and write it down:

Hard Decision:_____

If you don't have any hard decisions, well, good for you. If you have more than one, just start with the hardest one.

Trans-American Journey Analogy

Imagine your engine is making a funny noise, but the car still seems to run. While you ignore the noise, you can keep moving. You don't have to decide where to stop to get it looked at. By delaying the decision to fix the problem, you risk a much greater problem in the future.

→ # in summary

Make the big decisions now. Important decisions (the ones that will matter in a year) are the ones that tend to get overlooked. Don't overlook them.

5.10 Perspective

I love the concept of perspective. Here's one definition I found (yes, I did a little research, and it won't happen again): "Subjective evaluation of relative significance." Or put my way, "What's it mean? What's it matter?"

This book is about perspective. Putting your life in order is about looking at your life from the outside. We spend too much time being dragged along by the juggernaut of living, and too little time looking at the big picture of our lives. Hopefully this book is helping you redress the balance.

Perspective is about stopping and thinking. It's about looking at the relevance of a situation, the relative importance of events, and the consequences of decisions. What really matters? That's an important question. I'll ask it again. What really matters?

For some reason, many of us completely reverse the importance of things. I'll be doing something in my office (writing this book maybe) when my daughter wants to come and play with me. For some reason, I think the work is important and the playing is unimportant. For some reason, I think the football game I'm watching is important and talking to my wife is unimportant. Oh sure, you people know I'm wrong—when you look at the situation at arm's length. But at the time, that's not how it seems.

When choices occur in life (particularly when you are "busy"), take a moment to decide what is important and what isn't. Let me give you a helping hand. Anything to do with your family is generally important, and anything to do with work generally isn't. If you use that as a rule of thumb, you won't go far wrong. Try to project into the future the outcome of your actions. In ten years, will the people you sent all those emails to remember how important they were, or will your thirteen-year-old remember that dad was always too busy to play with her. Perspective is all about pausing, thinking, and predicting.

I'll give you an example that happened while I was writing this section. I was determined to get the first draft finished (we're near the end if you hadn't noticed). It was my day off and I woke up early with a view to getting into the office early to get stuck into writing. I was out of the shower by 6:30 a.m. and focused on the task at hand. When I got into the bedroom my four-year-old (at the time) was in our bed. My wife told me that our daughter was disappointed to find me out of bed because she wanted to play cards with me. (My father had taught her how to play poker and she was a little obsessed.) My first thought was to say, "Daddy has to go to work, honey." But I didn't. I used the perspective strategy. The thinking went like this:

Pause: I didn't say the first thing that came into my mind (which was, "Daddy has to go to work.")

Think: What were my options here? Go to work immediately or play cards for a few minutes.

Predict: What would be the consequences of either decision? If I went to work immediately, I would get an extra ten minutes of writing done and my daughter would be disappointed. Was it essential for me to go to work immediately? Would it matter if I was ten minutes late? What was more important, ten minutes of playing with my daughter or ten minutes of extra writing? I could always write later, but how often would I get to play with a four-year old? She wouldn't be four forever. Soon enough, playing with me wouldn't be a priority for her, even if it became more of a priority for me. So, the decision was easy. We played cards. Now, if I had a train or a plane to catch, or had no flexibility in my schedule, then maybe I would have disappointed her and made it up to her some other time. But that wasn't the case.

It's very easy to lose sight of what matters. Urgent things seem so important at the time, but how important are they in the greater scheme of things? If you're in the habit of worrying about lots of little things, you need a perspective strategy. The one I use goes like this: If I find myself becoming concerned about a decision, I think about what the consequences of a wrong decision will be in a day, in a week, in a month, in a year, or for the rest of my life. We talked about this before. It's good strategy for all aspects of your life, big and small.

If I'm tempted to be upset by something, I ask myself if the issue at hand will still upset me tomorrow. If the answer is no, then I wonder what the hell am I worrying about. Say someone stuffs up your coffee order. You're in a hurry and they give you a latte instead of a cappuccino. There's no time to correct the problem because you're in a hurry. Does this upset you? I've seen plenty of people upset by little things like this. Sure, it's annoying, but really? Will it be an issue in your life a day later? If the answer is yes, then you've got more problems than this little book is going to fix.

Say someone bumps into your car. How unhappy is that going to make you? It certainly is cause to be annoyed, but how annoyed? Will it matter in a day? Yes, it won't get fixed in a day. Will it matter in a week? Probably. Will it matter in a month? Probably not, because it will likely be fixed by then. It definitely won't be a problem in a year, so it's really not that big a deal.

If something is a going to be a problem in a year, then it is probably a real problem and you can worry about it if you want. If something is likely to be forgotten within a day, a week, or a month, then you should put it in perspective and put it behind you as quickly as possible. There are plenty of things in life that matter, so why spend time or emotional energy worrying about, being annoyed by, or concerned over things that will quickly be forgotten. Get a grip, people. Start exercising your sense of perspective and figure out what really matters. Focus on that.

Trans-American Journey Analogy

Don't just focus on the white line in the center of the road. Lift your gaze and take in the wider view.

in summary

Try to look at your life from the outside. Use the "pause, think, and predict" strategy to get decisions into perspective. Look at the consequences of your decisions and actions to determine what's worth worrying about and what's not. Focus more on the big picture and make time to reconsider impulsive thoughts. Will it matter in an hour, in a day, in a week, in a month, in a year, in five years? Choose your level of concern accordingly.

5.11 The 100 Percent Rule

I exposed the secret of writing earlier, when I revealed that books aren't written in a linear way. This book has required ideas to be pigeonholed into rules, challenges, or strategies. I didn't get these ideas in order. I'm not that smart. So, I'm comfortable enough (now that we know each other) to tell you that this is the last lesson I've learned before finishing the book, and it is just brilliant. God, I love serendipity.

There is joy in committing to something 100 percent. It gives you freedom and it gives you clarity. It simplifies decision making because you're giving something your full attention.

You know that feeling when you're reading a great book and you decide to forget everything else so you can finish it? At that point, you are invoking the 100 percent rule. You WILL finish the book at the exclusion of all else (except maybe bathroom breaks).

The 100 percent rule is not my idea, but when I read about it, a lot of things I'd observed but hadn't understood became clear. The concept is that 99 percent is hard, but 100 percent is easy. Put another way, the moment you wholeheartedly commit to something, it instantly becomes easier. The reason it becomes easier is because you automatically ignore the gravel and sand to focus on the rock. When you decide to finish reading that book, everything else will have to wait.

I mentioned before that when I got my cancer diagnosis, I decided to become a vegan. I got the diagnosis on a Friday and I was a vegan by Sunday. My friends were incredulous that I was able to do it, and they still secretly think I sneak meat every now and then (I don't). The 100 percent rule explains why it's been so easy. I don't eat meat EVER. Simple as that. I'm 100 percent committed. As a result, life is easier. I don't have to think about it. It's a rule and I follow that rule. The decision was made once very quickly, and I haven't wavered from that decision in the years since.

If I was "almost" committed to eliminating meat from my diet, then that would be hard. I'd have to decide if each circumstance should be classified as a "special occasion" during which I am allowed to break my rule. I expect this is why "social smokers" never quit. If you draw a line in the sand and commit to something 100 percent, then everything after that is easy. There is no turning back.

The way I see it, there are two "ways" to apply the 100 percent rule: 1) lifestyle changes and 2) projects. With lifestyle changes you can apply it multiple times at once. Maybe you're giving up coffee, or giving up sugar, or starting to floss your teeth before bed each night (sorry, had to slip that in). These are rules that don't take excessive time, but provided you are willing to commit 100 percent, you will easily be able to make the changes.

With projects, it's different. The 100 percent rule will allow you to complete a single project quicker than multiple projects at once. That's sort of the point. You give one thing 100 percent and get it done, and then you give another thing 100 percent and get that done.

The genius of the 100 percent rule is that you can apply it time and time again to get things done fast. Let me quote Susie Moore, who's article inspired me to apply the 100 percent rule:

> *True happiness is the joy we experience when we move toward our potential. The beautiful part is when we apply the 100 percent rule to a task at hand, we complete it. A project gets wrapped. A once-hopeful intention becomes a habit. A goal is met. It then frees up adequate mental space for the next priority to become clear, since we're not plagued by guilt about other multiple half-assed projects. And when we give 100 percent, other not-as-important stuff falls away in the meantime: It's an awesome perk to an already pretty-awesome rule.*

Nice work Susie. Well said. The 100 percent rule has allowed me to get the book finished. I'm excited now to attack other projects with the same gusto.

The 100 percent rule is a sprint, but you can't spend your entire life sprinting. Within the paradigm of my goal-setting model, it's a useful way to expedite projects or to commit to fundamental changes. I think you will miss out on the joy of the journey if all you do is apply the 100 percent rule in a serial manner (being 100 percent committed to project after project). Use it to get what you want (and you know what you want because you wrote it down in chapter 2, didn't you?), but don't over use it.

Trans-American Journey Analogy

The 100 percent rule is like overtaking a truck and a couple of cars on a narrow country road. You start out peacefully gazing at the scenery, before getting mildly frustrated at the slow progress. When you commit to overtaking the slow vehicles, everything else is ignored. Your attention is focused and you will not be distracted. For as long as it takes to get past that truck, you are 100 percent committed.

in summary

The moment you commit to something 100 percent it becomes easy. Why don't you commit now to applying the principles in the book? The decision to commit can be done in a millisecond, and then the rest of your life becomes simpler. Can you spare a millisecond to simplify your life?

Section 6

Spirituality
(Your Position in the Universe)

There's a lot to this life business, more than any of us realize. Actually, there's more to life than any of us are ever likely to comprehend, let alone realize.

There's a fine line between being a sceptic and being an idiot. We know so little of what there is to know in the world, so I find it difficult to discount the possibility of anything being true. That doesn't mean I think Uri Geller can really bend spoons with his mind, but it does mean that if someone has a paranormal experience, or something a little "out there," I'm not immediately dismissing them as being a lunatic. Let me quote myself here. I said this earlier, but it's worth saying again.

"Evidence does not define or display truth, it merely determines the current level of ignorance. Knowledge moves on. You can't be certain something is 'true.' Things just appear to be true given the available knowledge that can, in the fullness of time, be superseded."

We know so little of what there is to know that my standard position is that anything is possible. Anything.

Which brings me to God.

I've got to level with you. I've always had a problem with religion. Which one do you pick? I mean you wouldn't want to pick the wrong one, would you? I also have a problem with everyone who thinks their religion is the right one. It seems a bit arrogant to me. I don't have a problem with the idea of a God; it's just his/her middle management people that annoy me. The people running all the divisions of God Corp. are not necessarily doing it the way the Boss wants it done (or at least that's how it looks to me). I also have trouble believing God is a man. I'm going to use SHe now to make God androgynous. Please don't be offended. Just hear me out.

I think of God as the head of a big multinational company. God is chairman of the board, but not easily contactable. SHe's got a cell phone, but the reception is poor. All the division heads are running their bits of the business the way they think SHe wants it run. I'd hate to be one of those division heads who thinks it's a good idea to kill people from the other divisions when God finally fronts up for a board meeting. That's one review I wouldn't want to be part of.

I don't know if there IS a God, and you know what? It's so unlikely I'm ever going to know that it's ridiculous to worry about it. I have beliefs, of course. They are completely unsubstantiated beliefs and I'll never have proof. I know one thing, though. No one will ever be able to prove that God DOESN'T exist, so I'm all for keeping an open mind.

So, assuming anything is possible, and that God is possible, what does it all mean?

There are quite a few people I respect who do believe in God. They are very happy people to boot. There is a part of me that would love to be as happy as these people. If believing in God can make you that happy, then I'm all for it. The problem is, I don't believe in God the way those people do, and it's not something I feel I can force. I guess you either do or don't believe. You can't prove it, so you have to believe it. On occasion, I've felt like I was close to an understanding, but it never progressed.

I think the word "God" is a bit of a stumbling block for some people. I don't think of God as God. I think of God as being something greater and unexplainable, some underlying fabric of the universe, sort of like air. I can't see air, but I know it's there.

Let's not get caught up in semantics, however. For the purpose of this discussion, God is something out there that is more than we can ever explain or understand. I prefer to think in terms of spirituality more than God because people have this image of God in the white robe with the white beard sitting on the white cloud, whereas spirituality seems less defined, like fairy dust sprinkled through the universe. It isn't something you can see or touch, but sometimes you can sense it like a gentle breeze on your face.

Which brings me to my theory: God is a friend who will surprise you on your journey. There's no point picking up every rock looking for your friend. He or She will seek you out. You cannot force it. You have to let it happen. It will take many forms for many people. It is there. It can't be avoided, but it can be ignored. There is no point worrying what it is or who it is. God is like a good friend you have never met. One day you will turn around and SHe will smile at you and you will know. Don't go looking. You'll be found. It is a relationship that will change like all relationships. God is within.

I mentioned in the Serendipity section that Julian Hare, a patient of mine, offered up some interesting insights on this topic while I was inflicting him with a bit of oral carpentry.

Julian is a lapsing Catholic. He had a religious upbringing that he's spent many years reflecting on and refining. He believes in the duality of spirit and body. You start off all body and little spirit. As you journey through life you gain more spirit, until at the end you should be all spirit and no body (bye-bye, body). The purpose of life is the journey. Without the journey, you don't gain the experience to grow the spirit, which he feels is the whole point of existence. I like his ideas. Yes, I know someone probably had the idea before him, but because he told me he gets all the credit.

Julian's other idea I like is about the place for organized religion. He thinks the church should be like a parent. A parent prepares a child for life, for the journey. Basic needs are met, rules and values are explained, and at some point the parent loosens the grip and lets go. The child will have some spirit by that time (let's say twentyish) but the bulk of the task of seeking out and finding the spirit is ahead, unimpeded by the parent. He feels the church should do the same job: Prepare people for their spiritual journey, but don't endeavor to control the direction or nature of that journey. He sees the church as a parent that too often refuses to let go, and so stifles the growth of the child. If you let the church make decisions for you, then you never get to fulfill the potential of your spirit. You are always in the shadow of an overbearing parent. It's an idea worth considering if you don't feel your church fulfills you.

So, what is your position in the universe? I grew up in the Outback of Australia on a farm. During the final six months of high school, I commandeered the shearers quarters, which were about one hundred meters from the main homestead. Each night I'd have dinner with my family and then walk to the quarters to study and sleep. It had two rooms and a wood stove for heat. On my walk back each night, I would pause in the dark, away from the light of the homestead, and stare at the sky. I don't know if you've ever seen the night sky in the Outback of Australia, but it is truly something to behold. Spread out before you like a broad brush of white paint are the billions of stars of the Milky Way. You can't imagine the number of stars you can see, many of which are probably galaxies, not stars. Each night I would gaze at the universe spread out before me and contemplate my place in it. I've got to tell you, it was pretty demoralizing. It's hard to fathom that you (or anything else) matters when compared to the infinity of creation. It's hard to get motivated for an evening of quadratic equations after you've contemplated the majesty of the universe.

But contemplate we must. We all matter in our own universe. We're all here for a reason, even if getting here was as mundane as mum and dad's lack of birth control. We are all here, so why ARE we all here, and what are we supposed to do while we're here?

Remember that we discussed how you shouldn't worry about things you can't change or control? If your life isn't going to be complete until you learn the meaning of life, then it isn't going to be complete. Focus on what you can control and ignore the rest.

We are here and we need to make the most of it. You've got a journey to make between birth and death. Certain things will be revealed to you, and you will discover other things. You will learn no more or no less than you are supposed to learn. Your life matters as much to the universe as it's supposed to matter. Even the smallest bacterium has a purpose. It may not understand that purpose, but that doesn't remove the purpose.

Sure, I don't like thinking of myself as a proverbial bacterium in the colon of creation, but if I have no option, then what's it matter? In relation to the enormity of the universe, humans are like bacteria. I'm very grateful, however, for the fact that this little bacterium can have a hell of a good time while he's here.

This is one instance where I don't think perspective helps. Yes, we are inconsequential compared to the universe, but the universe can look after itself. My reality is that I'm here on Earth. I'm not planning any interstellar travel in the near future, so for all intents and purposes, this little blue-green planet **IS** my universe.

How important am I on Earth? Very bloody important if I'm any judge! I can impact positively on the lives of so many people in so many ways every day of every week of every month of every year I spend on Earth. That's a lot of positive energy I can project. And guess what? Everyone has that ability. Your universe is everyone you can affect. Even if we're all here for no reason at all, we can create a reason by making other people's lives better. That's a freaking fantastic reason for living if you ask me.

The more I think about Julian's ideas, the more I feel they coincide with my own. Life is a journey. What is the purpose of that journey? Julian wants your spirit to grow, and I don't have a problem with that. Maybe that IS the purpose of life. I want you to enjoy your life and do as much good as possible. It's hard to imagine your spirit not growing if you lived your life being happy and looking out for the other guy. It's hard to imagine God being unhappy with you if you lived your life being happy and looking out for the other guy. It's all about the journey, whichever way you look at it.

Will you find God on the journey? I don't know. I think with an open mind and an open heart you'll find exactly what you're supposed to find; or maybe more accurately, it will come and find you.

Trans-American Journey Analogy

The point of your journey is not the being there, it's the getting there.

➤in summary

I think there's something out there bigger than all of us, something that we will never be able to explain. There's no point worrying about finding it. Live a good life, and it will find you.

Epilogue

The time is not always right to be receptive to change. That old saying, "When the student is ready the teacher appears," or however it goes, is valid. The teacher is normally there, but the student is generally down at the back of the classroom asleep, or staring out the window in a trance. When they wake up, the lesson can be learned.

I have been asleep for much of my life, and I expect many of you have been asleep, too. Every now and then I'd wake up and learn something. It would normally take a crisis to wake me up, such as my wife leaving me, nearly going broke, almost dying—little stuff like that.

It would be nice if people didn't have to take themselves to the brink of oblivion to learn those important lessons. So, I hope you can learn from my experiences and make your life more enjoyable and peaceful. If this book doesn't mean anything to you now, then read it again next year. Hell, read it every year. It's not long. Maybe at some point in the future the student will be ready.

> "It's what you learn after
> you know it all that counts."

How true is that? I know enough to know I don't know much. This book has been a very honest attempt to determine what I think is important in life. Have I left bits out? Certainly. Is there something critically important

I've forgotten? Probably. If this book ever gets published, I'll probably write another one correcting all the mistakes that will inevitably be pointed out to me. I can live with that. It's what you learn after you know it all that counts. I love that line.

Live long and prosper.

About the Author

Brett Taylor is a frustrated author who ended up becoming a dentist. This is not to say he doesn't enjoy being a dentist. It's just that if Mr. McFadgen had encouraged him to pursue his dream in the ninth grade (instead of poo-pooing the idea) he might have embraced the whole writing thing forty years earlier. But I'm not bitter. Do I sound bitter? And how come now I'm writing in the first person when I started off in the second person? Do people really think someone apart from the author writes the "about the author section"? Seriously, think about it. You manage to write an entire book, and then you can't be bothered to write a few words about yourself?

But I digress. Things happen for a reason. I was given this life to make me think. I wouldn't change the course of my life, or all the challenging things that have happened in it, for anything. Life is a journey, which you now realize if you've read the book, or you will realize when you do. Author, dentist, father, husband, son, grandson, brother, uncle, nephew, cousin, patient, teacher, student, colleague, mentor, confidant, neighbor, and friend—like the rest of you, I'm many things, and much more than just the sum of my parts.

The author isn't just an author. And you (yes, I'm talking directly at you now) are also a whole a lot more than you think you are. Never forget that.

"Learn, love, amuse, and inspire." That's what I'm having chiseled on my headstone. I can think of worse ways to live a life. Get out there and live your life the best way you can, too.

If you go to *www.simplifyinglife.me* you can download the cheat sheet (right) to fill in while you are reading the book *Simplifying Life*.

Simplifying Life

1. Make Peace with the Past (put a big smiley face here when you've done it)

2. Goals (Choosing a Destination)

1 Family

Unrealistic Long-Term: _____

Realistic Long-Term: _____

Short-Term: One day _____ Date: _____

One week:_____ Date: _____

One month: _____ Date: _____

Birthday: _____

2 Health

Unrealistic Long-Term: _____

Realistic Long-Term: _____

Short-Term: One day _____ Date: _____

One week:_____ Date: _____

One month: _____ Date: _____

Birthday: _____

3 Career

Unrealistic Long-Term: _____

Realistic Long-Term: _____

Short-Term: One day _____   Date: _____

One week:_____   Date: _____

One month: _____   Date: _____

Birthday: _____

Goal Buddy _____

3. Attitudes and Actions (The Road Rules)

1. Pick good travelling companions

2. Compliment/encourage one person a day

3. Start writing Lifogies to: _____

4. Do something for someone

5. One belly laugh

6. Exultation   1._____   2._____

3._____   4._____

7. Anticipation 1._____   2._____

3._____

8. Tradition/rituals family_____

Tradition/rituals friends _____

9. Be happy where you are

10. Be open to serendipity

11. Be an inspiration

12. Give something (good) away

13. Live in the past now (reminiscing in the present)

14. Accept responsibility and move on

15. Put yourself in the other person's shoes

4. Challenges

1. Being negative

2. Being critical

3. Making compromises

4. Making excuses

5. Self-importance

6. Overcommitting time/money/emotion

7. Isolation

8. Expectation

9. Complacency

10. Comparing yourself to others

11. Distraction

12. Lack of challenges

5. Strategies

1. Prioritize tasks

2. Problem solving: 1._____   2. _____

3._____

3. Did I look at the worst-case scenario?

4. Was I true to myself?

5. Have I learned the lessons?

6. Apologize and move on

7. Compartmentalize your problems

8. Autopilot solutions to problems

9. Make the hard decisions now:

1._____   2. _____

3._____

10. Perspective

11. The 100 percent rule

6 Spirituality: Your Position in the Universe

Acknowledgments

I owe a debt of gratitude to everyone I've ever met, and a lot of people I've never met, for influencing my thinking. Given that's a long list, I'll just mention the major players in roughly the order they helped me.

First and foremost are my parents, Faye and Warren, who completely supported me for the first twenty-three years of my life, and then as required thereafter. My sister Kerry, grandparents, aunts, uncles, and cousins who helped shape my upbringing.

My friends Dave, Karen, Rod, Liz, Michael, Kerry, Mark, and Ulli, with whom we often eat, drink, and holiday. They have taught me the importance of anticipation and tradition. Actually, anyone I've ever planned a drink, meal, or BBQ with can be be thanked for teaching me about anticipation. Special mention to my neighbors Phil and Lyndall for their regular tuition.

My professional colleagues/friends Ammie, Andrew, Bill, Heidi, Ron, Mary-Jo, Omer and Marcie who have taught me the importance of being an inspiration. Ron gets a special mention for being one of the book's biggest fans. He kept me going when adversity stalled my progress.

My team at the office: Denise, Susan, Maria, and Amanda for supporting me (and putting up with me) day in day out for many years in my "real job."

My beta testers for challenging and encouraging me: Mark B, Mark D, Craig N, Fred G, Kelly Reed (RIP), Phillip, Prabu, Ellen, Dan, Diane,

Mike B, Jimbo, Grant R, Tim, Dave S, Don, Donna, Brad, Erich, Paul, Kit, and Mike W. Special mention to Mikey B for nailing the chapter 1 challenge.

My patients, for their confidence in me and for teaching me many things. In particular, Gary and Julian for their insights on religion.

My (sadly) deceased literary agent Ruth Wajnryb for being the first actual expert to believe my book was worthy of publishing (FYI no other literary agent thought so, and I gave a lot of them a chance). My editor, Glenn McMahan, for improving the clarity of my thinking and the organization of my ideas. The book is all that I wanted it to be thanks in no small part to his deft touch. My designer Rebecca Finkel for putting a face to my work. My computer genius mate Steve Brown for keeping you people on track with your goals.

The "guy" from Gulgong (real name Darren Gallagher) for reinforcing my views on serendipity, and reminding me that the journey never ends.

Lastly, and most importantly, my three gorgeous girls, Donna, Lauren, and Sophie. Donna is smarter than me and funnier than me, and makes my life worth living. Everything about her brings me joy. Lauren and Sophie have taught me more about life than they will ever realize. It has been a great privilege to watch them grow up, and I can't imagine how far they will go in life (and I'm pretty good at imagining). They are also both smarter than me, but I only think one of them is funnier than me. And I'm not saying who (smile).

Lastly (yes, really lastly now) I want to thank you, the reader. If a tree falls in the forest and no one is around to hear it, does it make a sound? I don't know to be honest. I do know that if someone writes a book and no one reads it, you will be able to hear the sound of the author softly crying under a tree in the distance. All books are a labor of love. If you're reading this, then you've made my labor worthwhile. So thanks.

Now, what are you waiting for? Get out there and live a great life.

Made in the USA
Columbia, SC
19 February 2018